Kingfisher first encyclopedia of animals

KINGFISHER

Editor Camilla Reid
Designers Steven Laurie, Ana Baillarguet

US editor Aimee Johnson
Proofreader Nikky Twyman

Photography Lyndon Parker, Andy Teare
Prop Organizer Michelle Callan
DTP Operator Primrose Burton

Artwork Archivist Wendy Allison
Assistant Artwork Archivist Steve Robinson
Picture Research Nic Dean

Production Controller Richard Waterhouse
US Production Manager Oonagh Phelan

Cover Design Jack Clucas

Writers John Farndon, Jon Kirkwood

Consultant Toby Stark
Specialist Consultant Andrew Kemp

**Produced for Kingfisher
by Warrender Grant Publications Ltd**

J
590·3

KINGFISHER

Kingfisher Publications Plc
New Penderel House
283–288 High Holborn
London WC1V 7HZ
www.kingfisherpub.com

First published by Kingfisher Publications Plc 1998
This edition first published by Kingfisher Publications Plc 2005

1 3 5 7 9 10 8 6 4 2
1TR/0505/TWP/*UP PICA(PICA)/150ENSO/F

A CIP catalogue record for this book is available from the British Library

ISBN-13: 978 0 7534 1191 9
ISBN-10: 0 7534 1191 1

Printed in Singapore

Your book

Your *First Encyclopedia of Animals* is the perfect way of finding out all about the exciting world of animals. Packed with fascinating information, interesting activities and brilliant pictures, it can be used for school projects or just for fun.

◁ The information about each picture is printed next to it. The arrows show you which information goes with which picture.

◁ Some pictures follow a sequence. Watch out for the numbers to make sure you follow them in the right order.

▽ Step-by-step instructions show you how to do the activities.

Fact box
• These boxes contain extra information, facts and figures.

▷ Labels on some pictures give extra information about the animal. These labels show the points of the horse.

mane   forelock
withers
hindquarters
tail   shoulder
hock
fetlock   hoof

Find out more
If you want to find out more about each topic, look at this box. It will tell you which pages to look at.

Contents

Animal Lives

Habitat

A habitat is the place where an animal lives. It provides the animal with food, water and shelter – everything it needs to survive. There are many different habitats all over the world.

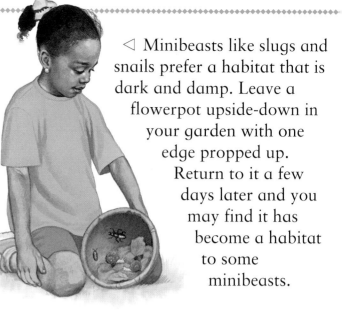

◁ Minibeasts like slugs and snails prefer a habitat that is dark and damp. Leave a flowerpot upside-down in your garden with one edge propped up. Return to it a few days later and you may find it has become a habitat to some minibeasts.

savanna

rainforest

desert

△ Over millions of years, animals have evolved to survive in their own habitats. For example, the camel is able to live in the desert because it can go for days without drinking. If a habitat changes – for example, if the rainfall decreases – each animal must adapt to the new environment. Unlike humans, if an animal is suddenly taken out of its habitat it cannot adapt quickly enough and is unlikely to survive.

Find out more
Camel
Chimpanzee
Evolution
Giraffe

Migration

Many animals make journeys from one place to another to find better living conditions. Some move quite short distances, but others travel from one side of the world to the other. These regular return trips are known as migration.

▷ In autumn, you may see 'V' formations of Canada geese flying overhead. Make a note of when they leave and in which direction they go. Watch for their return in spring.

▽ The Earth is criss-crossed with animal migration routes. Use the colour-keyed arrows on the map to see where these four migrating species travel each year.

■ Canada geese (above) fly to the Arctic Circle in the spring to breed. In autumn, they return to warmer southern regions.

■ Grey whales spend the winter in the warm sea off California, where they give birth to their calves. In summer, they swim north to the rich food supplies in Alaskan waters.

■ Arctic terns travel further than any other animal. Each year, they move from pole to pole and back again.

■ Swifts spend the summer in Europe, where they catch insects to feed their young. They spend the winter in Africa.

◁ Many grass-eating animals in Africa migrate to find food. Like these wildebeest, they follow the rain as it moves.

Find out more
Arctic tern
Reindeer
Swift and
Swallow
Whale

Defence

A fast animal can run away from a predator but slower animals need other methods of defence. Thick armour and sharp spines will deter many attackers, as will nasty poisons and bright colours. Other animals simply hide and hope for the best!

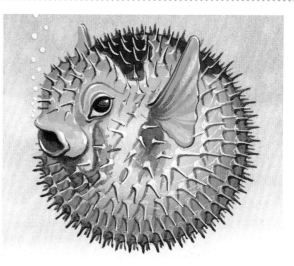

△ The porcupine fish inflates its body to make its spines stand out. This will put off most attackers.

◁ The octopus hides in a hole and changes colour to blend into the rock. If spotted, it spreads out its tentacles to make itself look huge and frightening.

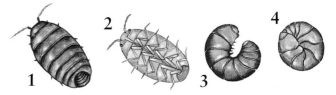

1 2 3 4

△ The woodlouse defends itself by rolling into a ball so its tough, outer body is all an enemy can see.

▷ A game of hide and seek is very like a hunt between a predator and its prey. The hider will try to make herself as small as possible so that the seeker does not see or hear her.

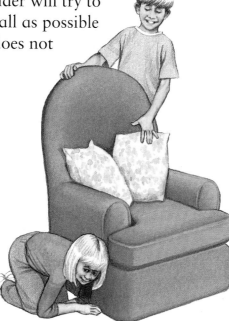

Fact box

• Animals with a sting or poison are often brightly coloured and have stripes. Predators learn to avoid them.
• Lots of animals use camouflage to hide.

△ A shell acts like a coat of armour for a tortoise. When danger threatens, it pulls its head and legs inside the shell until it is safe to come out.

Find out more

Armadillo
Baby animal
Camouflage
Turtle and Tortoise

Camouflage

Many animals use camouflage – body shapes, colours or markings that help them to blend in with their background. Camouflage helps animals hide when hunting or being hunted.

△ The tiger's stripes help it blend in with the tall grass on the sunny, open plain where it lives. This makes the tiger hard to spot as it waits to ambush its prey.

◁ The plaice hides by lying flat on the seabed and changing colour to match the sand and pebbles.

▷ Leaf insects look almost the same as a leaf. They also move slowly to try to fool predators into thinking they are leaves. Even their eggs are leaf-shaped.

△ **1** Play a camouflage game with some friends. First you need to find three or four everyday objects, such as a tin, a bottle and a carton. Then stick leaves, grass and scraps of paper to them. Finally, paint them with brown or green paint.

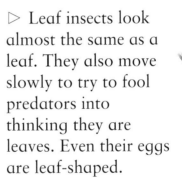

▷ **2** Take the objects into the garden and put them among the plants. Tell your friends what you have hidden and challenge them to find the objects. The person who finds the most things wins.

Find out more
Chameleon
Evolution
Tiger
Zebra

11

Food

All animals need to eat in order to survive. Animals that eat plants are called herbivores; those that eat meat are carnivores. A chain of living things that eat each other is called a food chain.

◁ **1** A mobile is a good way of showing how a food chain works. Cut out shapes of an owl, a mouse and a lump of grain from pieces of coloured card.

▷ **2** The mouse eats the grain and the owl eats the mouse. So hang the grain inside the mouse, and the mouse inside the owl. Connect the shapes with pieces of thread.

△ This puma has killed a deer. Once the puma has eaten its fill, the remains will be food for vultures, ravens, coyotes and maggots.

▷ There are many different food chains. One food chain in the sea starts with phytoplankton. These tiny plants make their food from sunshine.

phytoplankton

copepods

herring

cod

△ Nothing is wasted in a food chain. Even the smallest scraps of dead animal will be food for another creature.

killer whale

harbour seal

◁ Each animal is eaten by a bigger one. The killer whale is at the top of this particular food chain. So, indirectly, it gets its food from the tiny phytoplankton.

Find out more
Defence
Killer whale
Owl
Vulture

Conservation

Many animals are in danger of dying out, or becoming extinct. This may be because their habitat has been destroyed or polluted, or because they have been hunted. It is important that we conserve these animals and their homes.

△ Rubbish pollutes the environment. It is also dangerous to animals, who may get trapped inside empty cans and bottles. Collecting rubbish is an excellent way of helping animals.

△ Corncrakes nest in farm fields, and normal farming methods kill them. Special ways of harvesting may help more of them survive.

◁ Dodos once lived on the island of Mauritius, but because they could not fly they were easily hunted by sailors visiting the island. In 1680, the dodo became extinct.

▽ In the last 50 years the survival of whales has been threatened by over-hunting. Nowadays, whale hunting is carefully controlled.

Find out more
Antelope
Lemur
Panda
Tiger
Whale

Communication

Animals communicate with each other for many reasons – for example, to find a mate, to warn of danger or to scare other creatures away. They have many different ways of sending these signals to each other.

friendly   playful

ready to defend   ready to attack

◁ Wolves communicate with each other using facial expressions. These four expressions carry very different messages.

△ Fireflies are beetles that use light to send signals. The light comes from special cells in their abdomens. The fireflies flash their lights to attract mates and to warn off predators.

▽ To hoot like an owl, clasp your hands together and blow between your thumbs. Do it outside at night and an owl might hoot back at you!

△ Moths communicate using smell. The female gives off a scent and the male picks it up using his feathery antennae.

Find out more

Beetle

Butterfly and Moth

Owl

Wolf

Reproduction

From the huge whale to the tiny ant, all animals must reproduce (make babies) so that their species can survive. There are many different ways of doing this.

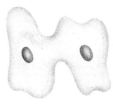

△ The amoeba is a microscopic animal made of just one cell. Its way of reproducing is very simple – it splits in half. The new cells will reproduce in the same way.

▽ **1** When two birds mate, the male fertilizes an egg inside the female. The female lays the egg, and a chick starts to grow. **2** As it grows, the chick feeds off the egg white and yolk. **3, 4** When it is ready to hatch, the chick pecks at the eggshell and breaks out.

△ The babies of almost all mammals grow inside their mothers and are born live. They must be fed and protected until they can look after themselves.

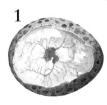

◁ You can help birds bring up their young by putting up a nesting box on a tree or a building. Make sure it is between two and five metres above the ground. Keep a note of the changes that you see.

▷ While most reproduction needs a male and a female, earthworms are both male and female at once. The thick saddle in the middle of the body produces eggs that can be fertilized by any other worm.

saddle

Find out more
Alligator and
Crocodile
Baby animal
Bird
Mammal

Baby animal

When they are young, many animals need looking after, just as human babies do. Their parents must keep them safe from harm and find food for them until they are old enough to look after themselves.

△ When danger threatens, the male mouthbreeder fish shelters his young in his mouth. He spits them out as soon as it is safe.

△ The merganser duck sometimes gives its babies a piggyback. This keeps them safe until they are old enough to swim by themselves.

△ A zebra foal must learn to walk straight after it is born so it can follow its mother away from danger. The male zebras will protect the herd by kicking and biting any attackers.

△ Emperor penguins keep their babies warm by carrying them on their feet.

◁ Play the baby penguin game with four or more people. Divide into two teams and stand in rows. The aim is to pass a bean-bag along each row using only your feet. The first team to get the bean-bag along the row wins.

Find out more

Alligator and Crocodile

Gorilla

Mammal

Penguin

Reptile

Evolution

Millions of years have passed since life first started on Earth. The animals that lived then are very different from those that are found now. This is because things evolve (change) over a long time to stand a better chance of survival.

△ **1** Fossils are the remains of animals that died millions of years ago. They are a good way of telling how things have evolved. You can find fossils on some beaches and in certain types of rock formations.

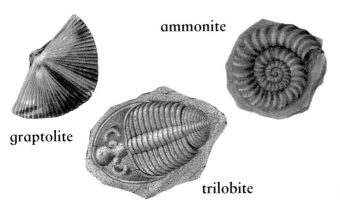

ammonite

graptolite

trilobite

△ **2** Look at fossils with a magnifying glass. You will see that they look quite similar to some animals still alive today. The way they have changed shows how they have evolved in order to survive.

◁ Once there was just one type of fox, but new forms evolved. The Arctic fox has thick fur to keep warm, and is coloured white for camouflage.

▷ The desert fox has evolved to deal with the hot desert. It has large ears to help it keep cool, and is sandy in colour.

◁ The peppered moth has evolved very recently. Usually this moth is light coloured but a black-winged form is found in places where the trees have been blackened by smoke from factories. This gives it better camouflage.

Find out more
Bird
Camouflage
Defence
Habitat

Mammals

Mammal

Mammals are a group of animals that includes humans. They are warm-blooded vertebrates and are found all over the world – in the water, on the land and in the air. There are 4,000 species of mammal and they all have certain features in common.

△ A human and a cat are both mammals. They are each covered in hair or fur and they both have a jaw-bone joint which only mammals have.

△ Mammals can be carnivores (meat-eaters), herbivores (plant-eaters) or omnivores (meat- and plant-eaters). This bushbaby is an omnivore that belongs to the primates, a group of mammals that are able to grasp objects with their hands.

▽ All mammals feed their young on milk produced by the female. Apart from animals such as the platypus, all mammals give birth to live young.

▷ Because mammals are warm-blooded, they keep the same body temperature no matter how hot or cold the surroundings. Ask an adult to help you measure your temperature in a warm place and then in a cold place. It should always stay close to 37 degrees centigrade.

Find out more
Baby animal
Evolution
Rabbit and Hare
Reproduction

Lion

Lions are the largest predators in Africa. These powerful big cats live in groups called prides in bush country or on grassy plains. A pride is made up of several females and their cubs, as well as a few males. Apart from humans, the lion has no enemies and is known as the 'king of the beasts'.

▽ Lions hunt mainly at night and spend the day resting. They prey on many of the large animals of the plains, including antelope, zebra and buffalo. As well as looking after the cubs, the lionesses (female lions) do most of the hunting.

△ The male lion has a large, shaggy mane around its neck. It is his job to defend the territory of his pride and he will warn off intruders with a loud roar. Adult lions have thick tawny-coloured coats, while lion cubs have spots.

Find out more

Cat (wild)
Cheetah
Leopard
Mammal
Tiger

Tiger

Tigers are the biggest of all cats. They live in the grasslands and forests of Asia, where their striped coat gives them good camouflage when they hunt.

△ Female tigers give birth to between one and three cubs. The cubs stay with their mother for over a year.

△ A tiger slowly stalks its prey, a deer, through the long grass. When it is close enough, it makes a sudden dash, leaps onto the deer's back and knocks it down. A quick bite to the neck kills the deer.

◁ Tigers are hunted for their beautiful coats, and for their bones and body parts, which are used in traditional Chinese medicine. Because of this, tigers are nearly extinct.

Find out more
Cat (wild)
Cheetah
Leopard
Lion

Leopard

Leopards are the most common of all the big cats. They live in forests, deserts, mountains and grasslands, and are found in Africa, India and Asia. They have become rarer in India and Asia because they have been hunted for their striking, spotted coats.

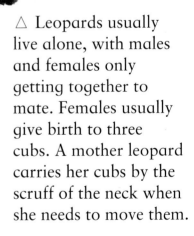

▷ Leopards are strong animals and good climbers. They carry prey up trees to keep it from scavengers. Leopards hunt gazelles, pigs and monkeys, but eat birds and insects if there is nothing else to eat.

△ Leopards usually live alone, with males and females only getting together to mate. Females usually give birth to three cubs. A mother leopard carries her cubs by the scruff of the neck when she needs to move them.

◁ Leopards are great swimmers and love being in water to play and to hunt. In wet areas, like highland and tropical forests, leopards have black fur. These leopards are called panthers.

Find out more
Cheetah
Lion
Mammal
Tiger

Cheetah

Cheetahs are slim, spotted cats with long legs. They are the fastest land animals and can reach speeds of over 100 kilometres per hour. Cheetahs are found in the open plains of Africa, south of the Sahara.

△ Cheetahs can only run at high speed for a short distance They bring down their prey by tripping them up.

◁ Female cheetahs have up to four babies at a time. The cubs have a long coat of grey hair, which makes them look like honey badgers. Honey badgers are aggressive animals so other animals will not go near them. This 'disguise' keeps the cubs safe from harm.

Fact box
• Cheetahs are the only cats that cannot draw their claws back fully. They use them to grip while sprinting after prey.
• A cheetah's body measures 1.4m and its tail is 80cm long.

▷ Cheetahs once lived in North Africa, the Middle East and India. But they have been trapped and tamed in Asia, and are now seriously endangered. Cheetahs are also rare in Africa.

Find out more
Cat (wild)
Leopard
Lion
Mammal
Tiger

Cat (wild)

Apart from the big cats like lions and tigers, most wild members of the cat family are fairly small. Many wild cats are hunted for their boldly patterned coats. Because of this, some are in real danger of extinction and need protection in the wild.

▽ Caracals are cats that live in dry, scrubland areas of India and Africa. They particularly like to eat birds and will often leap up to catch them. The saying 'Putting the cat among the pigeons' comes from the actions of this cat.

△ The European wildcat is found in forests from western Asia, through the continent of Europe, to Scotland. They are nocturnal animals that hunt birds and small mammals for food. The female gives birth to between three and six kittens.

Fact box

• The smallest cat is the rusty-spotted cat, at just 35 centimetres long. It lives in India.
• The fishing cat of India has webbed paws.
• European wildcats can be 40 centimetres at the shoulder and weigh up to ten kilograms.

△ The North American bobcat gets its name from its short (bobbed) tail. It lives in forests and deserts and catches rabbits, mice and squirrels.

Find out more

Cat (domestic)
Leopard
Lion
Tiger

Elephant

Elephants are the heaviest land animals. They are also intelligent and have good memories. There are two species: one lives in Africa, the other in India. They use their long trunks almost like an arm, to put food and water in their mouths. Their tusks are made of ivory and males use them for fighting.

△ In India, elephants are trained to do heavy work, such as lifting logs. An elephant driver or keeper is called a mahout.

◁ **1** The African elephant is bigger than its Indian cousin. It has bigger tusks and ears and a hollow forehead. The tusks are really teeth that grow outside the mouth.

◁ **2** The Indian elephant has smaller ears and a rounded forehead. Only the male Indian elephant has tusks.

▽ In Africa, elephants live in small family groups ruled by the oldest females. Males live in all-male herds.

1

2

Fact box
• African elephants grow to four metres, over twice as tall as an adult human.
• They weigh as much as seven tonnes – heavier than six cars.
• Elephants can live to be 70.

Find out more
Giraffe
Hippopotamus
Rhinoceros

Zebra

Closely related to horses, zebras are grazing mammals that live on the grasslands of Africa, south of the Sahara desert. Their striped coats make it hard for other animals to spot them. Even if they are seen, zebras can run faster than most of their predators.

△ Zebras live in family groups with one stallion (male), several mares (females) and their foals (young). If threatened by a lion, the mares lead the foals to safety, while the stallion kicks out with his powerful back legs.

Fact box

• Zebras are smaller than horses: 2.2m long and 1.3m tall.
• Young females leave the family at two years old. They must then search for a new family to join.
• Males leave the family at four years old.

△ When there is plenty of grass to eat and water to drink, several zebra families may join together to form a large herd. If food becomes scarce, the herd may migrate long distances to find new grasslands, sometimes crossing wide rivers.

△ Zebra stripes are like our fingerprints – no two patterns are the same. Grevy's zebra (above) has much finer stripes than the mountain zebra.

Find out more
Antelope
Donkey
Giraffe
Horse

Rhinoceros

Rhinoceroses (or rhinos) are large, heavy animals that live on open grassland in Asia and Africa. They are protected from predators by tough, armoured skin and sharp horns. Although rhino horn is very hard, it is actually made of a material similar to hair.

△ Rhinos weigh up to five tonnes and can charge at 50 kilometres per hour.

▽ Rhinos have poor eyesight, but a very good sense of smell. Females with young calves are likely to charge if they feel threatened by an unfamiliar sound or scent, and males are often bad-tempered. But rhinos will let birds called oxpeckers ride on their backs and feed on the insects living on the rhino's tough skin.

Indian rhino   African white rhino   African black rhino

△ African rhinos have two horns; Asian rhinos have one. Indian rhinos have a long upper lip for eating reeds and grass. The white rhino, which is actually grey, has a wide upper lip for grazing. The black rhino uses its pointed upper lip to eat leaves.

Find out more
Elephant
Hippopotamus
Horse
Pig

Hippopotamus

These huge animals have large barrel-shaped bodies and short legs. The name hippopotamus comes from Greek and means 'river horse'. Although they are not related to horses, they do live near rivers – in Africa.

▷ Hippos spend the day in the water with just their eyes, nose and ears showing. This stops them getting sunburnt. They can stay underwater for up to ten minutes before having to come up for air.

Fact box

• Hippos live in groups of up to 15 in rivers, lakes and ponds across Africa.
• They can grow to 4.6 metres long, stand 1.5 metres at the shoulder and weigh as much as 4.5 tonnes.
• Hippos are related to pigs.

△ Hippos have gigantic mouths with two huge tusks on the bottom jaw. In the breeding season, competing males show off the size of their mouths and may cut each other with their tusks. Hippos leave the water at night and travel to look for the grasses they eat. They have hard lips, which they use to cut the grass.

◁ Baby hippos can weigh 55 kilograms at birth. They can stand within minutes of being born, and must keep close to their mother for protection.

Find out more
Horse
Pig
Rhinoceros

Buffalo

Buffalo are big, strong, dark-coloured mammals with huge horns. African buffalo live in herds of several hundred – usually near water, as they love to wallow in mud. Water buffalo are found in the wetter areas of Asia. Few are found in the wild now and they are mostly kept as farm animals.

△ African buffalo have very bad tempers, so humans have never managed to tame them.

Fact box

• When looking for insects, egrets (right) use buffalo as perches.
• The horns of the water buffalo are the biggest in the animal kingdom.
• Like cows, buffalo chew their cud, bringing once-eaten food back up for a second chew.

△ Males are much larger than females. Their horns meet together as a lump on their heads. This helps protect them from any attack. Groups of lions attack females and young, but they will rarely go for a male.

◁ Water buffalo have been domesticated for 3,000 years. They are used to pull carts and ploughs, but they can be kept for their meat, milk and hides. Only a few survive in the wild in Asia, but buffalo released in Australia now run free in the swamps of the Northern Territory.

Find out more
Cow and Bull
Mammal

Dog (wild)

In many ways wild dogs look and behave like domestic dogs, and they are related. However, wild dogs are usually afraid of humans and cannot be trained. These meat-eaters often live in packs and are found all over the world.

▷ Like most wild dogs, the Cape hunting dogs of East Africa are fierce killers. They have long front teeth for piercing or tearing, and sharp cheek teeth for slicing meat into small chunks. They work in teams to chase down antelope, zebra and wildebeest.

◁ Wild dogs rely on their sense of smell and sharp hearing for hunting. Once they have found their prey's scent, they give chase. Like other dogs, North American coyotes (left) howl to call up the pack for a hunt.

Fact box

• The dhole of India can kill bears and even tigers.
• Golden jackals of southeastern Europe now live mostly on human rubbish.
• The coyote is sometimes called the prairie wolf.

◁ Jackals live in Africa and Asia. They hunt mainly alone at night, and form packs only when there is a chance of sharing a lion's kill.

Find out more

Dog (domestic)

Fox

Wolf

Wolf

Wolves are the largest of the wild dogs. They are natural hunters that work in packs when tracking their prey. Because of their sharp fangs and spooky howl, many people are afraid of wolves and believe that they will attack humans. But humans are rarely on their menu.

△ Wolves have long been hunted by humans. They are now found only in the remote northern areas of Asia, Europe and North America.

◁ Wolves live in family groups headed by one or two lead wolves. Young wolves are energetic animals and spend much of their time play-fighting. When they are older, they are taught to hunt by their parents.

▽ The wolf pack will chase its prey until it is exhausted and easier to capture. They hunt various animals, from small rodents to reindeer and musk oxen.

Find out more
Dog (wild)
Fox
Mammal
Reindeer

Fox

Foxes are small wild dogs with short legs and big, bushy tails. They are skilful hunters that come out at night and rest by day in burrows called dens. The female is called a vixen, the male is a dog and the young are cubs.

good hearing

sharp eyesight

excellent sense of smell

△ The red fox lives in woodland and feeds on small animals, insects and fruit. Foxes living near towns may scavenge from dustbins.

◁ Foxes are found in most parts of the world. The fennec fox lives in the deserts of North Africa and the Middle East. During the day it stays below ground in its burrow to avoid the heat of the sun. Its huge ears also help it to lose heat and to keep cool.

▷ Foxes' pointed ears give them very good hearing. This helps them detect the slightest noise of a small animal in the grass. Roll two pieces of card into cones and hold them to your ears. Get a friend to make a noise behind you, then hear for yourself the difference with the cones and without.

Find out more

Dog (domestic)
Dog (wild)
Wolf

Giraffe

Giraffes are the world's tallest animals, measuring up to six metres. Their front legs are so long that they have to spread them wide apart in order to drink at water holes.

▽ Giraffes live in small family groups on the African plains. About 15 months after mating the female giraffe gives birth to a calf. The calf can get onto its feet and follow its mother only an hour or two after being born.

◁ The spotted pattern on its coat helps to hide the giraffe from its enemies. Spots can be big (above), or blotchy (left). Each giraffe has a different pattern.

△ Giraffes use their height to graze on the leaves at the top of acacia thorn trees. The giraffe tears off the spiky twigs in its tough mouth. It can also curl its long tongue round even higher branches and pull them down to its mouth.

Find out more

Antelope
Buffalo
Zebra

Camel

Camels live in the world's driest deserts. They have humps of fat on their backs that help them survive for days without food or water.

▽ A camel's feet are big and wide to stop it from sinking into the desert sand.

△ Camels have been used since ancient times to carry people across deserts.

△ A camel has two rows of eyelashes to shield its eyes in a sandstorm. It can also close its nostrils tight.

◁ The Arabian camel, or dromedary, has one hump. The Bactrian camel has two humps. Bactrians live in Central Asia; dromedaries live in North Africa, the Middle East and India.

Find out more
Antelope
Cow and Bull
Giraffe
Llama

Llama

The llama is found in the high Andes mountains and on the dry plains of South America. Like its relative, the alpaca, it is tame. They are both relatives of the wild guanaco. All three are members of the camel family.

△ Guanacos usually live on mountains over 4,000 metres high, although they are also found on the lower plains. Their blood is rich in red cells, which helps them to breathe the thin mountain air.

△ Today, llamas are used mainly as pack animals, as they were by the ancient Inca people of Peru. Female llamas are used for meat, but the males are too tough to eat.

▷ Alpaca wool is prized by the local South American people. It has a soft feel and provides warmth in the cold climate.

Find out more
Camel
Goat
Mammal
Sheep

Antelope

Antelopes graze on the wide plains of Africa and Asia and can run fast. There are many different types of antelope. They range in size from the royal antelope, which is 25 centimetres at the shoulder, to the giant eland, which is 1.75 metres tall. Male antelopes, and sometimes females, have curved horns.

▽ The addax is a rare antelope that lives in the Sahara. Its horns are long and twisted. Its hooves are broad to help it walk on soft sand.

◁ Wildebeest, or gnu, are antelopes that migrate in huge herds of up to 500,000. They follow the rain to find rich pastures. Wildebeest are the most common wild grazing animals in East Africa.

▷ Oryx have long, sharp horns and black-and-white faces. They live in the deserts of the Middle East and Africa. Two oryx species, the Arabian and the scimitar oryx, have been hunted until there are very few left in the wild.

◁ Springboks are small, graceful antelopes that live on the open plains of southern Africa. These animals, which have bold markings, can be 80 centimetres tall. Their name comes from the way they leap, or spring, into the air.

Find out more
Camel
Deer
Llama
Reindeer
Zebra

Deer

Deer come in all shapes and sizes, from the tiny puda to the large moose. They are graceful mammals that can run swiftly from danger. Deer are found in the Northern Hemisphere as well as in South America.

△ 1 Make a cast of a deer hoof-print to keep forever. First take a piece of card six centimetres wide and 50 centimetres long. Bend the card into a circle around the hoofprint and fasten with tape.

△ 2 Mix some plaster of Paris powder with water to make a thick paste. Pour the paste into the card mould until it reaches just below the top of the card.

△ Each year, male deer grow a new set of antlers. During the breeding season, they fight fierce battles with each other for the position of leader of the herd.

△ 3 Leave it until it sets hard, then carefully lift off the plaster in its mould. Take home your cast and remove the card. Using an old toothbrush, clean off any soil from the plaster cast.

Find out more
Antelope
Mammal
Reindeer

Reindeer

Reindeer are found in the Arctic regions of Asia, Europe and North America. They live on the tundra (plains) and in forests. The reindeer is closely related to the caribou of North America.

▽ Like all other deer, reindeer lose their antlers in spring, then grow a new set that reaches full size in autumn. Reindeer are the only deer where the females have antlers like this males.

△ Reindeer feed on grass, lichens and twigs. In the winter they use their large hooves to shovel the snow away to dig for food. In winter their thick coats are grey; in summer they are brown.

▽ People first tamed reindeer over 3,000 years ago, and they have been used as transport and for their meat and fur ever since. However, people have never managed to tame caribou in the same way.

◁ Reindeer and caribou migrate over long distances. They move south in the autumn and north in the spring. Young or weak animals are often preyed on by hungry wolves.

Find out more
Deer
Mammal
Migration
Wolf

Bear

The bear is the largest meat-eating animal on Earth. There are many kinds of bear and most of them live in northern parts of the world. Their thick fur coats protect them from the cold.

Kodiak bear

brown bear

polar bear

black bear

△ Most bears are large and powerful, with strong claws and a good sense of smell. The Kodiak bear of Alaska is the largest of all. It weighs almost 700 kilograms and, when standing up, can be four metres tall.

◁ In winter, some bears find a snug place to hibernate. Hibernation is a very deep sleep that may last many weeks. The workings of the bear's body slow down to save energy.

◁ In the autumn, American black bears hunt salmon and eat berries and honey. This helps them to put on the weight they need in order to survive their long hibernation.

Find out more
Mammal
Polar bear
Raccoon

Panda

The giant panda is a bear found in just a few high bamboo forests in China. There are probably no more than 1,600 giant pandas left in the wild. About 140 are kept in zoos around the world.

▽ Pandas have one or two cubs at a time. At birth, a cub weighs only 100 grams. At first the mother holds it close to her chest at all times. But it grows quickly and after ten weeks the cub starts to crawl.

△ Giant pandas usually only eat bamboo. To help them grasp the stems, they have an extra pad on their front paws that works like a thumb. Giant pandas have become rare since their forests have been cut down and because they were once hunted for their fur.

▷ Red pandas look very much like raccoons. They live high up in the mountain forests of the Himalayas, from Nepal to China. They feed at night on roots, acorns, bamboo and fruits.

Find out more
Bear
Mammal
Polar bear
Raccoon

Polar bear

Polar bears live in the frozen regions of the Arctic, where they hunt and raise their young. Their white fur makes them almost invisible in the snow. They mainly feed on seals, but also eat fish, geese and ducks. They are the only northern bears that do not hibernate in the winter.

△ Polar bears have thick, oily coats and a layer of fat to protect them from the icy temperatures, which can drop to –30°C.

◁ Polar bears are good swimmers – they have to be to cross the moving packs of ice. They are often found swimming in the sea many kilometres away from an ice pack or land. Their large, furry feet make good paddles for swimming.

△ Polar bears often wait at the breathing holes of seals. When the seal comes up for air, the bear catches it, kills it and then eats it.

Fact box

- Male polar bears weigh up to 800 kilograms.
- Baby polar bears are born in winter in ice dens. They stay in these with their mothers until it gets warmer.

◁ Polar bears live alone and only meet when they go south to mate. They go as far as the mouth of the Amur River in Russia and the Gulf of St Lawrence in Canada.

Find out more
Bear
Penguin
Seal and Sea lion

Orang-utan

The word orang-utan means 'man of the forest' in the Malay language, and it is true that this large ape does look a bit like an old, hairy man. Orang-utans live in the rainforests of Southeast Asia.

Fact box
• Male orang-utans weigh up to 90kg and may grow to be 1.5m tall.
• In the wild, orang-utans live about 35 years.
• When it rains, orang-utans often use a large leaf as an umbrella.

▷ Baby orang-utans are reared by their mothers and will stay with them until they are around five years old.

△ Orang-utans have become rare partly because their forest habitat has been cut down, but also because some people think baby orang-utans make good pets, and steal them from the wild. Mothers are often killed while defending their babies.

▽ Orang-utans have long, strong arms. They climb slowly through the trees in the morning and evening searching for wild figs – their favourite food. At night they sleep on platforms made of branches.

Find out more
Baboon
Chimpanzee
Gorilla
Monkey

Gorilla

Gorillas are huge and powerful apes. They look fierce, but are actually gentle vegetarians. They are now very rare and are found only in the forests and mountains of Central Africa.

▽ Gorillas live in family groups. These are led by a big male called a silverback, who gets his name from the silver hairs on his back. These hairs grow when a male gorilla is about ten years old. Silverbacks may be as tall as a man and weigh 225 kilograms – about three times as much as a man.

△ Gorillas eat leaves and buds, stalks, berries and sometimes even tree bark. When they have eaten most of the food in one place, they move on to let the plants grow back again.

◁▽ Gorillas learn to walk at about ten months. They feed on their mother's milk for the first two years and spend much of their time playing. They sleep with their mothers until they are three years old, then they make their own nests of leaves and branches.

Find out more
Baboon
Chimpanzee
Monkey
Orang-utan

Chimpanzee

Chimpanzees, or chimps, are our closest animal relatives, and are some of the most intelligent animals. They live in tropical rainforests and woodlands in Africa. Chimps eat fruits, leaves and seeds, but they also like termites and ants.

△ Chimps sometimes use twigs to prise insects out of their mounds, and will crack nuts open by hitting them with stones.

Fact box

• The tallest male chimps are about 1.6m tall when they stand up – almost as big as a small human adult. Female chimps are shorter.
• Chimps can live to be 60 years old.
• Chimps live in groups. These have between 15 and 80 members.

△ Chimps spend a lot of their time in trees. They use their long arms to swing from branch to branch in search of food. At night, they build nests of leaves to sleep in.

◁ Chimps usually move about on all fours, but they can also walk upright, which leaves their hands free. If attacked, a chimp may defend itself by throwing stones.

Find out more

Baboon
Gorilla
Lemur
Monkey
Orang-utan

Baboon

Baboons are large monkeys that live in troops of over 100 in number. They feed on many different foods, from seeds, fruits and grasses to small animals and eggs. They are found in the Middle East and in Africa, south of the Sahara.

△ Baboons spend much of their time grooming each other. This helps form bonds between babies and mothers, and also between members of the troop. The troop is usually made up of related females, males and one lead male.

▽ Mandrills, from the West African rainforests, are cousins of the baboon. They have bare patches on their large faces. In adult males, these are brightly coloured.

▷ The gelada is a monkey similar to a baboon that is found in the mountains of Ethiopia, in East Africa. It has a hairless red patch in the centre of its chest, from which it gets its other name – the 'bleeding heart baboon'. The males have very long hair over their head and shoulders.

Fact box

• Baboons sometimes weigh 40kg. They can be 1.15m long, and have tails 70cm long.
• Male baboons are twice as big as females.
• Baboons bark like dogs when frightened.

Find out more
Chimpanzee
Gorilla
Monkey
Orang-utan

Monkey

Monkeys are clever mammals that can solve problems and hold things in their hands. They live in groups called troops, high in the tropical forests of the Americas, Africa and Asia. Monkeys eat plants, birds' eggs, small animals and insects.

△ A monkey's eyes face forwards, which helps it to see well when hunting. Most monkeys hunt by day.

△ Howler monkeys come from South America and are good climbers. They use their tails as an extra 'hand' when swinging through the branches. Howler monkeys live in groups headed by an old male. They get their name from the loud calls the group makes together to warn off other monkeys from their territory.

▷ The capuchin monkey is a small monkey that lives in the Amazon jungle. Because of its intelligence and curious nature, it is often kept as a pet and taught to do tricks.

Fact box
• One difference between monkeys and apes is that monkeys have tails, while apes do not.
• A female monkey usually has one baby or, sometimes, twins.

▽ The proboscis monkey of Borneo gets its name from its big nose. It has a long tail too, but uses it only for balance.

Find out more
Baboon
Chimpanzee
Gorilla
Lemur
Orang-utann

Lemur

Lemurs live only on the forested island of Madagascar off the coast of Africa. They are rare because the forests where they live are being destroyed by farmers. Although lemurs look like monkeys with their long tails, they belong to a different family.

▷ Most lemurs spend their time high up in the trees, but the ring-tailed lemur is often found on the ground. It is the only lemur to have a striped tail, which it uses to signal to other lemurs.

▽ The rare indri is the biggest lemur and may reach 1.3 metres high. It is unusual because it comes out during the day to find food, and has only a tiny stump for a tail.

Fact box

• Lemurs are primates like apes, monkeys and humans.
• Most lemurs like to eat fruit and leaves, but they also eat insects and eggs.
• The smallest lemur is the mouse lemur, at only 15cm long. Most lemurs are around 60cm.

△ Like most lemurs, the aye-aye is active at night, using its big eyes and ears to find food and sense danger. It has an extra-long middle finger on each front paw. It uses this to hook insects and grubs out of holes in trees and to spoon them into its mouth.

Find out more
Chimpanzee
Gorilla
Monkey
Orang-utan

Kangaroo and Wallaby

Kangaroos and wallabies are marsupials that live in Australia. Marsupial females have pouches on their bellies in which their babies can grow until they are big enough to survive on their own.

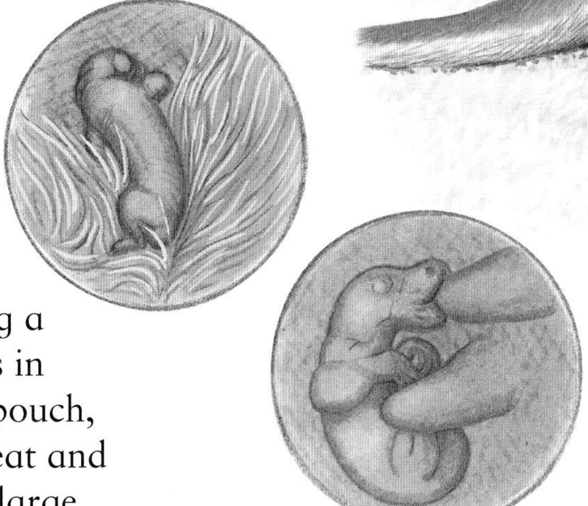

▷ A baby kangaroo is called a joey. When it is born, the baby is just two centimetres long. It crawls up to the mother's pouch along a path the mother licks in her fur. Once in the pouch, the joey clings to a teat and stays there until it is large enough to look after itself.

△ There are 56 species of kangaroo and wallaby (the name given to the smaller kangaroos). Most live on the ground, but some live in trees.

▷ Kangaroos are brilliant jumpers. They bound along on their strong back legs, using their long tails for balance. They can jump over ten metres in one leap.

Find out more
Koala, Wombat and Opossum
Mammal
Platypus

Koala, Wombat and Opossum

Koalas live in the eucalyptus forests of eastern Australia. Because they look a little like bears, they are sometimes called koala bears. However, they are marsupials, not bears. Wombats and opossums are also marsupials.

△ Wombats look like koalas, and also live in Australia. But they are larger – between 70 and 120 centimetres long – and live on the ground. During the day they stay in the grassy nests that they make at the end of their long burrows. They come out at night to feed on grasses and the roots of shrubs and trees.

▽ The only marsupials to live outside Australia are opossums, which are found in North and South America. A typical opossum grows to about 100 centimetres long. At least half its length is its hairless tail, which it uses to grip things.

△ When a young koala leaves its mother's pouch, it rides on her back. Koalas spend all their lives in the tops of eucalyptus trees eating the leaves and bark. They only come down to cross to another clump of trees.

Find out more
Kangaroo and Wallaby
Mammal
Platypus

Raccoon

The striped tail and black mask of the North American raccoon make it easy to spot. Raccoons are forest creatures, but they have learned to scavenge from humans and often make their dens near towns.

△ People's rubbish makes a tasty lunch for a raccoon. Raccoons will often get used to humans and can be partly tamed. However, they will always keep their wild instincts and may be fierce fighters.

Fact box

• The raccoon gets its name from a Native American word that means 'scratches with hands'.
• There are seven raccoon species.
• Wild raccoons live for about five years.

△ Even though they are weaned at two months, young raccoons are protected by their mother for up to a year.

▷ In the wild, raccoons eat berries, acorns and seeds. They like to live near rivers so they can hunt for crabs, frogs and fish. They also rinse any dirty food in the water. When the young are old enough, they leave their mother to live on their own.

Find out more
Bear
Beaver
Fox
Panda

Beaver

Beavers live near rivers in North America and northern Europe. They are great builders and use their massive front teeth to cut down trees. Beavers use these trees to make their homes, which are called lodges.

Fact box

- Beaver dams can be over 500m long and up to 4m high.
- Some beaver dams are 1,000 years old.
- A male and female pair of beavers will stay together for their whole lives.

△ Beavers dam the river with branches to make a pond. In this pond they build a lodge. Beavers use their large, webbed feet and big flat tails to push themselves through the water. If alarmed, they slap their tails on the water to warn other beavers.

◁ Beaver lodges are made of sticks and mud. Beavers seal their lodges with more mud during the winter. The mud freezes hard and helps to keep out predators.

▽ The adults enter the lodge by an underwater entrance and bring food to their young hidden inside. The young beavers will stay with their family for about two years. Then they leave to build their own lodges.

lodge

dam

Find out more

Mouse
Otter
Rabbit and Hare
Rat

Badger

Badgers are powerful creatures, but they are also shy. They are related to skunks and, like them, have black and white markings. In Europe, they live in family groups in woodlands.

▽ Badgers are omnivores, which means that they eat all kinds of food. Their diet includes grasses, fruit and nuts, as well as small animals and eggs. They are good at digging and often catch earthworms.

▽ Badgers are most active in the evening. This is when they come out to feed and to collect straw for bedding.

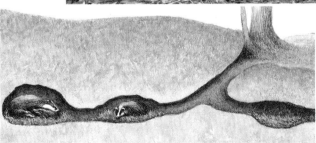

◁ During the day, badgers stay in burrows called setts. As the group of badgers grows bigger, they dig more underground chambers. Some large setts have been used for hundreds of years.

▷ Unlike the European badger, the American badger lives alone for most of the year in dry, open countryside. It also has a different face pattern.

Find out more
Food
Mole
Skunk

Mole

Moles are small mammals that spend almost all their lives underground. We know they are around because of the molehills they create when digging their tunnels. They live in Europe, Asia and North America.

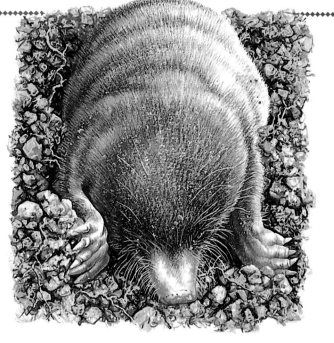

△ Big, powerful front paws, a pointed nose and sharp claws mean that moles are excellent diggers. Although they have bad eyesight, they hunt for worms and insects using their good sense of smell and by picking up vibrations with their whiskers.

△ Baby moles are born in a nest, called a fortress, deep below a molehill. They are lucky to be born at all – like all moles, their parents fought furiously when they first met.

◁ When moles dig tunnels they push the earth to the surface, which makes molehills. These are more common in autumn, when young moles look for new areas to live.

Fact box
- Moles surface at night to search for nest material.
- The star-nosed mole has a star of sensitive fleshy tentacles on its nose.
- People used to make clothes from mole fur.

◁ Golden moles are found in dry places in Africa. They live underground and burrow through sand to find food. Like all moles, they have very soft and silky coats.

Find out more
Badger
Mammal
Mouse
Worm

Armadillo

Armadillos are armour-plated mammals related to anteaters and sloths. They are found in regions of North America and all through South America. There are 20 species in all – the largest is the giant armadillo, which is 1.5 metres long.

△ Armadillos live alone, in pairs, or in small groups in burrows. They come out at night to feed. They are easily frightened and bolt for their burrows when threatened.

◁ Armadillos eat many different kinds of plants, insects and small animals. They are fond of ants and termites, which they dig up with their powerful front legs and claws.

▽ When in danger, armadillos roll up into a ball, showing only the hard plates on their head and tail.

Fact box

• Despite their heavy armour, armadillos swim well. To help them float, they swallow air.
• The smallest armadillo is the pink fairy armadillo, which is 16cm long.
• The most common is the nine-banded armadillo.

Find out more

Aardvark
Ant and Termite
Defence
Hedgehog
Mammal

Aardvark

The aardvark is an African mammal that eats termites and ants. Its hearing is so sharp that it can detect these insects moving underground.

◁ The aardvark tears away at termite nests to get at the juicy insects inside. Once the galleries and chambers of the nest are opened up, it quickly licks up the termites.

◁ The word aardvark means 'earth pig' in the Afrikaans language. This name was given to them by Dutch settlers in Africa. Aardvarks are the same size as pigs but they have much larger ears and longer snouts.

◁ Inside the aardvark's huge snout there is a 30-centimetre long, sticky tongue. It is perfect for probing into insect mounds.

◁ Aardvarks live in burrows under the ground. If threatened by a lion, they use their strong claws to dig themselves a deep hole in which to hide.

Find out more
Ant and Termite
Lion

Meerkat

Meerkats are small meat-eating mammals. The word meerkat means 'marsh cat'. However, they actually live on the dry, open plains of Africa, not on marshes. They are known for their comic way of standing on their hind legs, on the lookout for predators.

△ Meerkats live in burrows under the ground. They come out during the day to hunt for food, but they are always watching out for eagles and other birds of prey.

▽ Meerkats often hunt by digging for prey with their long, sharp claws. They also look for insects, eggs, small animals and plant roots to eat. They have a good sense of smell, and can see and hear well.

△ Like the meerkat, the mongoose will often attack poisonous snakes, in order to defend its burrow and its young.

Find out more
Cat (wild)
Cobra
Eagle
Mammal

Skunk

Skunks live in woods and grassland in North and South America. They have long, furry tails and black-and-white fur. They are known for the foul smell they give off in defence.

△ Skunks have around three babies in the spring. The young are born blind and do not leave the burrow for six weeks. When fully grown, they leave to find their own home.

△ Skunks are about the size of domestic cats, and weigh up to three kilograms. They rest in their burrows by day, and come out at night to find plants, birds' eggs, insects and small mammals to eat.

▷ The skunk has a special way of dealing with a predator such as a lynx. First it thumps its paws on the ground. Then it turns round, flinging up its rear legs to expose its bottom.

Fact box
• The commonest skunk in North America is the striped skunk.
• The other two types are the hog-nosed skunk and the spotted skunk.
• Skunks can spray an attacker from a distance of 4m. The smell lasts for days.

▷ If the attacker does not heed the warning, the skunk lowers its legs and squirts a jet of liquid from glands near the tail. The smell is so awful that few predators return for more.

Find out more
Badger
Defence
Otter

Squirrel

Most squirrels have big, bushy tails and live in trees. They are active during the day, running from branch to branch in search of nuts, fruit and seeds.

▷ The red squirrel, like the one seen here, is smaller than its grey cousin. In Britain, red squirrels are being forced from their woodland homes by the more aggressive grey squirrels, which were imported from North America about 100 years ago.

▽ The prairie dog is a burrowing squirrel that lives on North American grasslands. Their large underground burrows, called towns, contain up to 1,000 prairie dogs.

◁ Squirrels love seeds like acorns, which they gnaw with their sharp front teeth. In autumn, they sometimes bury a supply in the ground to last them through the winter.

Find out more

Habitat

Mammal

Mouse

Rat

Reproduction

Mouse

Mice are small rodents with long tails and sharp front teeth. These grow all the time, so mice must gnaw things to stop them from getting too long. There are many kinds of wild mouse, found all over the world. Mice can also be kept as pets.

△ Mice eat many foods, including seeds, grain, roots, fruit and insects. They also enjoy human food. The house mouse lives in people's homes.

△ American harvest mice are good at climbing. They build globe-shaped nests above the ground on the stems of grasses.

▽ Mice breed very quickly to make up for their short life spans. Baby mice are born naked, deaf and blind, but they look like small versions of their parents after only two weeks and female mice are able to breed when they are just six weeks old. In one year, a female mouse can have more than ten litters of up to twelve babies.

◁ Dormice live in Europe, Africa and Asia. Unlike many other mice, they have furry tails. Dormice make nests from plants and, in cold places, sleep through winter.

Find out more
Beaver
Food
Guinea pig, Gerbil and Hamster
Rat

Hedgehog

Hedgehogs are mammals found in the woods and hedges of Europe, Asia and Africa. Most have thousands of thick spines covering their backs, which help to protect them from predators. There are also hairy hedgehogs, which live in Asia.

▽ The common hedgehog usually has about four babies. The babies do not get pricked when they drink their mother's milk as she only has spines on her back. Adults go out after dark to hunt for food. They will eat plants, but prefer insects and frogs.

Fact box
• Babies are born blind, with soft spines.
• Hedgehogs spend more than 20 hours a day sleeping. In cold northern regions, they hibernate in winter, curling up under a pile of leaves.
• One hedgehog, the moon rat of Sumatra, can be 40cm long.

△ Hedgehogs can be friendly, especially if you leave them some dog or cat food. It is best not to touch them, though, as they often carry fleas.

△ When a hedgehog senses danger, it curls up into a tight ball with its spines on the outside. This puts off most predators, although many hedgehogs are killed by cars when they curl up on roads. They are able to climb trees and, if they fall, the spines act as a cushion.

Find out more
Defence
Fox
Mole
Porcupine

Porcupine

Porcupines are covered in spines called quills and this makes them look very much like hedgehogs. However, the two are not related. Porcupines are actually rodents and they have large teeth for gnawing.

△ When a porcupine is threatened, it raises and rattles its quills. If the warning is ignored, the porcupine backs into the attacker and jabs its sharp quills into the animal's flesh.

△ Young porcupines are born with soft quills. As adults, porcupines are about 90 centimetres in length.

▷ Most porcupines have long quills, but the quills of the North American porcupine are short. It lives mainly in forests but also wanders into open countryside. North American porcupines climb trees to feed on leaves, berries and bark, and often strip enough bark from a tree to kill it.

Find out more

Beaver

Hedgehog

Rat

Rat

Rats are rodents with sharp teeth, furry bodies and long tails. There are over 120 types of rat, living all over the world. The brown rat and the black rat are the most common.

△ Brown rats and black rats originally came from Asia, but they are now found all over the world, wherever humans live. It is said that there is probably one rat for every person on the planet.

△ Both black and brown female rats will have between six and 22 babies in a litter. They can have up to seven litters a year.

▷ Pack rats, also called wood rats, are American rodents that live in nests made of plants. They are nocturnal and eat grasses and cereals.

Fact box

• Rats can carry about 30 diseases affecting humans.
• In the Middle Ages, one in four Europeans died from the plague – a disease spread by rats.
• Rats have been known to gnaw through electric cables!

▷ Humans see rats as pests because they spread disease and spoil human foods. They are intelligent animals and will use their sharp teeth to bite through most obstacles.

Find out more

Beaver

Guinea pig, Gerbil and Hamster

Mouse

Guinea pig, Gerbil and Hamster

Guinea pigs, gerbils and hamsters are all mammals. These rodents live wild in many parts of the world, but they also make very good pets. They need a good-sized cage and should be given food and water every day. They also enjoy lots of care and attention.

Fact box

• Hamsters are originally from Europe and Asia; guinea pigs, from South America; and gerbils, from Africa and Asia.
• Guinea pigs were taken to Europe as long ago as the 1500s.
• Despite their name, guinea pigs are not related to pigs.

▽ In South America, humans have been eating guinea pig meat for about 4,000 years. Wild guinea pigs, called cavies, still live on the grasslands there.

△ Guinea pigs feed on grass and green plants in the wild, so if you give them dry pet food, make sure they have plenty of water.

▽ Hamsters live alone and come out at night to eat grasses, seeds and berries. They have big pouches in their cheeks that they use to carry food back to their nests.

▷ Gerbils live on the edges of hot deserts. They hide in burrows by day and come out at night to feed on seeds and insects. Their long back legs and tails help them to leap across the hot, sandy ground.

Find out more
Beaver
Mouse
Rabbit and Hare
Rat
Squirrel

Rabbit and Hare

Rabbits and hares are closely related. Hares are bigger than rabbits and have longer ears and legs. Hares live above ground, while rabbits live underground in linked-up tunnels called warrens.

△ The black-tailed jack rabbit of the hot North American deserts is really a hare. Its very long ears help it to cool down in the fierce heat of the day.

△ Rabbits were originally found in the countries around the Mediterranean Sea. Humans have now introduced them to countries around the world.

▽ Rabbits are popular pets. They are friendly animals and easy to keep in outdoor hutches. They need to be fed and watered every day and their hutches must be cleaned regularly.

Fact box

• Rabbits have up to ten babies in a litter and give birth seven times a year.
• Young hares are called leverets.
• Top speed for a hare is 56 kilometres per hour.

Find out more

Guinea pig, Gerbil and Hamster

Rat

Squirrel

Walrus

Walruses are sea mammals that live along the edges of the ice in the cold Arctic waters of the Atlantic and Pacific Oceans. Both males and females have two long, white, ivory tusks. Their wrinkled skin covers a thick layer of blubber (fat) that helps to keep them warm.

△ Walruses like to sun themselves for a while before plunging back into the freezing Arctic waters. They may form large colonies on beaches. In the past, large numbers of walruses were killed for meat, for oil and for their tusks. Today they are a protected species and are growing in number.

△ Like sea lions, walruses walk on land by turning their flippers under their body and can support themselves on all four limbs.

▷ Walrus tusks are up to 40 centimetres long. Males use their tusks to defend themselves and to fight over females. Both sexes also use their tusks to haul themselves onto the ice and to dig for their food – shellfish, which they find by using their bristly whiskers.

Find out more
Dolphin
Mammal
Seal and Sea lion
Whale

Otter

Otters are mammals that are found near rivers and seashores around the world. Although the otter makes its home on the land, it spends much of its time in the water.

△ Female otters give birth to between one and five young in an underground burrow called a holt.

long tail: this acts like as ship's rudder to steer the otter

fur: two layers keep the otter warm and dry

eyes and nose: on top of the head so the otter can see and breathe while swimming

whiskers: help the otter feel movements in the water

teeth: long, sharp teeth grip and bite prey and crack shells

feet: webbed feet for swimming fast

claws: sharp claws help the otter to dig

▷ Otters eat fish and small animals. They are strong swimmers and well designed for hunting in the water.

▽ Young otters spend lots of time playing and wrestling with each other. One of their favourite games is to slide down a snow or mud bank.

△ Sea otters are found along the northern rim of the Pacific Ocean – from California to northern Japan. They often float on their backs and sometimes carry their young on their bellies.

Find out more
Beaver
Mammal
Platypus
Seal and Sea lion

Seal and Sea lion

Seals and sea lions are good swimmers and divers. They are mammals so they have to come up to breathe, but they can stay underwater for up to 30 minutes. They feed on fish and penguins.

▽ While sea lions can walk on their flippers, seals cannot. Male sea lions have thick fur on their necks that looks like the mane of a lion.

▽ Seals catch their prey underwater, then they come to the surface to eat it.

◁ Female seals and sea lions suckle (feed) their babies on milk that is extremely nourishing. The milk is full of fat and helps the babies grow quickly.

▽ Male elephant seals are the largest seals in the world. They get their name from their floppy noses, which look like trunks.

Fact box

• The Baikal seal of Russia is the only freshwater seal in the world.
• Sea lion colonies sometimes have hundreds of thousands of sea lions in them.
• Monk seals are one of the few species to live in tropical water, such as the Caribbean Sea.

Find out more
Dolphin
Killer whale
Mammal
Whale

Killer whale

Killer whales are the largest members of the dolphin family. They are powerful hunters and can be up to ten metres in length. Killer whales have strong jaws and teeth. They eat fish, dolphins, seals – even other whales.

▽ Killer whales find their way and track their prey by sending out little clicks of sound, then picking up the echo. They live in families called pods. Usually there are ten or so in a pod, but there may be up to 100. Like all whales, killer whales are mammals and give birth to live young.

Fact box
• Killer whales sometimes launch themselves onto a beach to catch seals resting near to the water line.
• One killer whale caught in the Bering Sea had 32 seals in its stomach.
• Killer whales have never killed, or even attacked, humans.

△ Killer whales are fast swimmers, with rounded flippers and strong tails. They can swim at over 55 kilometres per hour, and can jump high out of the water. They live in most of the world's oceans, near the North and South Poles.

Find out more
Dolphin
Food
Shark
Whale

Whale

Whales are the biggest creatures that have ever lived on Earth – even bigger than dinosaurs. Like dolphins, whales are mammals and breathe through blowholes on their backs. They are found in all the oceans of the world.

△ The blue whale is the largest animal on Earth. It measures up to 30 metres long and weighs 100 tonnes – as much as 15 elephants.

△ Humpback whales are known for their booming songs. This is how they 'talk' to each other. The songs can be heard hundreds of kilometres away. These whales often leap right out of the water in the mating season. Sometimes a male and female will hold each other in their long flippers.

Fact box
• Blue whale babies are seven metres long when they are born.
• Sperm whales can hold their breath for about 70 minutes.
• Many whales feed on one of the smallest creatures in the sea – the shrimp-like krill.

◁ Sperm whales eat giant squid. They hunt them deep under the sea – over 450 metres down. The whale's skin has scars on it from the battles between these huge animals.

Find out more
Dolphin
Killer whale
Octopus and Squid

Dolphin

Dolphins are intelligent, graceful sea creatures. They are not fish, but mammals and, like us, they breathe air. They make clicking sounds to help them find their way, catch their prey and communicate.

white-sided dolphin

△ There are over 30 species of dolphin, found in seas all over the world.

Fact box
• A dolphin's top speed is 40 kilometres per hour.
• A dolphin breathes through a blowhole in the top of its head.

spotted dolphin

◁ Dolphins send out sounds in pulses. Then they listen for echoes bounced back from nearby objects to find out what is around them. This way, they can track down fish to eat.

▽ Bottle-nosed dolphins love to play. Like many other dolphin species, their streamlined shape and powerful tails help them speed through the water and they often jump high into the air. They live in big family groups called schools, and like to race alongside boats.

bottle-nosed dolphin

Find out more
Killer whale
Whale

Platypus

The platypus is a strange animal. It is part of a small group of animals called monotremes, which have features of both mammals and reptiles. It has a beaver's tail, a duck's bill and webbed feet. Like a reptile, it lays eggs, but it gives milk to its young, just as mammals do.

△ The platypus is found in Australia and Tasmania. Like the otter, the platypus lives in a burrow and hunts in the water.

◁ The platypus has fur similar to an otter's. Even its flat tail is covered in fur. When swimming, the platypus paddles with its front feet and steers with its back feet and tail. It uses its sensitive, rubbery bill to find food in the muddy beds of the rivers and lakes where it lives. Platypuses eat crayfish, shrimp, worms, frogs and small fish. They need to eat their own weight in food every day.

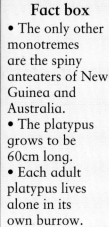

Fact box
- The only other monotremes are the spiny anteaters of New Guinea and Australia.
- The platypus grows to be 60cm long.
- Each adult platypus lives alone in its own burrow.

▷ Before laying her eggs, the female platypus makes a nest at the end of her burrow. She lays two or three eggs, then seals the opening of the tunnel to stop predators entering.

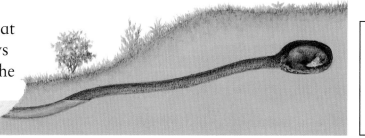

Find out more
Beaver
Otter
Shrimp and Prawn

Bat

Bats have big ears, furry bodies and wings like leather. They are nocturnal mammals. This means they sleep in caves and attics during the day and fly out to feed at night-time.

▽ Bats are the only mammals that can fly. They are very fast and acrobatic. When they chase after insects, they twist and turn in mid-air.

△ Bats use sound to catch insects in the darkness. They send out high-pitched squeals that humans cannot hear. The echoes that bounce back tell the bats exactly where they will find their prey.

Fact box
• The 'bumblebee', or hog-nosed, ` bat may be the world's smallest mammal. It is only two centimetres long.
• The South American vampire bat feeds on the blood of living animals.

▷ Flying foxes, or fruit bats, are large bats that live in tropical Africa and Asia. They mainly eat fruit. Flying foxes are important because they help to spread the pollen and seeds of many plants.

Find out more
Bird
Insect
Mouse

Dog (domestic)

Dogs were domesticated about 12,000 years ago, when cavemen first tamed the Asiatic wolf. Since then, dogs have lived with people wherever they have travelled. They have been bred to help people both in their everyday lives and in their work.

Bernese mountain dog

▷ There are about 400 dog breeds, which are divided into seven groups. These are: sporting dogs, hounds, working dogs, terriers, toy dogs, non-sporting dogs and herding dogs. The Bernese mountain dog is a working dog, the Labrador is a sporting dog and the Yorkshire terrier is a toy dog.

Yorkshire terrier

Labrador

▽▷ The collie (below) and the corgi (right) are both herding dogs. Collies help to round up sheep. Corgis once helped to herd cattle. Many collies work on farms, but most corgis are now just pets.

△ Dogs kept as pets should be taught to walk on a lead and house-trained. They must be looked after properly throughout their lives.

Find out more
Cat (domestic)
Dog (wild)
Fox
Mammal
Wolf

Cat (domestic)

All the domestic or house cats of today are descended from wild cats. They were first tamed over 4,000 years ago in ancient Egypt. Although domestic cats are fed by humans, they are still hunters like their ancestors, and have the same sharp teeth, pointed claws and sensitive eyes for seeing in the dark.

tortoiseshell

blue tabby

chocolate point Siamese

▷ There are now over 40 different 'breeds' of cat. Some, like the Siamese, have short hair. Others, like Persian cats, are long haired.

◁ Cats make good pets, as they are clean, quiet and friendly. They can be quite independent but still need to be well cared for. Kittens have to be trained so that they become used to humans and learn good habits in the home. They enjoy human contact, especially being stroked.

▷ The African wildcat is probably the domestic cat's main ancestor, although other cats have also been taken from the wild and tamed by humans. African wildcats look like domestic tabbies, but they are slightly bigger. Their fur is also thicker and the markings are not as bold.

African wildcat

domestic cat

Find out more
Cat (wild)
Cheetah
Leopard
Lion
Mammal
Tiger

75

Goat

Goats are hardy and good at climbing, and they can survive in the highest mountains. Wild goats are found across the Northern Hemisphere. Tame goats are kept for their milk, meat and skin.

feral goat

Cretan wild goat

Apennine mountain goat

△ Kashmir and Angora goats are valued for their fine wool. The long, silky coat of the Angora (above) gives mohair or angora wool. Kashmir goats give cashmere wool.

△ Goats were first tamed 10,000 years ago, and there are now many breeds. They like to eat grass and plants, but they will eat almost anything and can survive on thorn trees and shrubs. Male goats are often bad-tempered and use their long, curved horns to fight each other for females.

▽ Ibexes are wild goats found in Europe, Africa and Asia. They live on the mountaintops in summer, and move to warmer, lower pastures in winter.

Fact box

• Goats' hooves have hard edges and soft centres. They act like suckers on steep, slippery rocks.
• Goats give off a very strong smell.
• A young goat is called a kid, a female is a doe or a nanny, and a male is a billy.

Find out more
Antelope
Cow and Bull
Mammal
Sheep

Cow and Bull

Female cattle are called cows and the males are called bulls. They are kept on farms all over the world for their meat, called beef, and for their milk. We also use their hides (skin) to make leather shoes and clothes.

Friesian cow

Jersey cow

Hereford bull

Highland cow

△ Female cattle that are reared for their milk are called dairy cows. Twice a day they are brought in from the fields to be milked. Special machines suck the milk from the cow's udder.

△ Although they are not clever animals, cattle are very strong. In many parts of the world, they are used to pull ploughs and carts.

△ There are over 250 breeds of cattle, and each has its own qualities. Friesians give a lot of milk. Jerseys are famous for their rich, creamy milk. Herefords are often used as beef cattle. Highland cattle are tough enough to survive cold winters.

Find out more
Buffalo
Mammal
Pig
Sheep

Sheep

Sheep were first tamed in the Middle East over 7,000 years ago. They are kept all over the world for their wool, meat and skins. Female sheep are called ewes, males are called rams and the young are called lambs.

Hampshire down

Southdown

Romney

Scottish black face

△ Farm sheep can have two or three lambs at a time. Some newborn lambs are very weak and may need to be hand-reared. Wild sheep only give birth to one lamb.

◁ Today there are about 700 million sheep on farms all over the world. There are more than 800 breeds, each suiting different climates and producing different types of wool.

▷ Wild sheep have hairy coats to protect them from the cold mountain climate. In winter, they grow a thick undercoat of fine wool called fleece, which falls out (moults) in spring. Farm sheep are sheared before they moult, giving us wool.

Find out more
Cow and Bull
Goat
Mammal
Pig

Horse

Long legs, a big heart and large lungs make horses strong and fast – which is why people have used them to ride and to pull carts for 5,000 years. Horses are descended from wild horses that once lived in herds on grassy plains.

dun

dark bay

roan

light bay

palomino

piebald

chestnut

skewbald

grey

black

▷ Horses come in many colours, each with a special name.

◁ Ponies can be kept as family pets. They need a field to live in, and lots of care and attention. They should be exercised regularly and need their hooves trimmed every few weeks.

▽ Grooming keeps a pony's coat glossy and healthy. Be sure never to walk behind a horse or pony – it may kick out in surprise.

▽ Every part, or point, of a horse has a name. Horses are measured in hands. One hand is four inches (about ten centimetres) – the width of a man's hand.

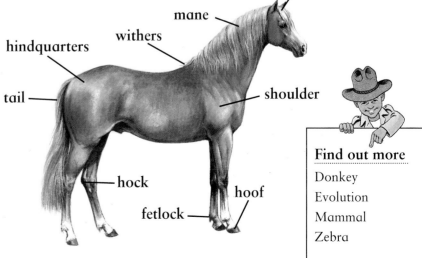

forelock

mane

withers

hindquarters

tail

shoulder

hock

fetlock

hoof

Find out more
Donkey
Evolution
Mammal
Zebra

Donkey

Patient and strong, donkeys are used all over the world to carry people and goods. Their small feet and thick coats make them suited to working in dry, rocky places. Because they are quiet animals and gentle with young children, donkeys are often kept as pets.

▽ Donkeys range in colour from almost white to nearly black. They usually have two dark stripes running along their backs and across their shoulders. Unlike horses, only the ends of their tails have long hairs.

▽ Donkeys are descended from wild asses that were tamed by the ancient Egyptians. Wild asses look very similar to donkeys, with large pointed ears and small hooves. They have thin black stripes on their legs, unlike donkeys.

▽ Donkeys are usually good workers. They can also be stubborn and will make a loud braying noise if they are angry or upset.

Find out more

Horse

Zebra

Pig

Pigs were first tamed 9,000 years ago in China. Today most pigs are farm animals, raised for their meat and skins. Pigs eat almost anything. They are intelligent animals and some people keep them as pets.

△ There are over 90 breeds of tame pig. They grow very quickly and, when raised on a special diet, may grow to two metres in length in just two years.

△▷ Baby pigs are called piglets. The mother pig, called a sow, usually has a litter of up to 12, and has two rows of teats along her belly from which the piglets drink milk. Sometimes the weakest piglet, called a runt, is not able to feed and needs to be looked after by a human.

▽ Wild boars are fierce animals that live in forests in many countries. The piglets have stripy coats that help to camouflage them.

Find out more
Camouflage
Goat
Mammal
Sheep

Birds

Bird

Birds live all over the world and there are nearly 10,000 species. They are the only animals to have feathers and wings, but not all can fly. All birds lay eggs, and most build nests where they can raise their chicks.

◁ Most birds, like this magpie, have a very light skeleton, strong chest muscles, a tough beak and eyes on the side of the head. Nearly all birds make sounds, called songs, to 'talk' to each other.

▷ Birds have evolved to fit the places where they live and the foods they eat. Birds of prey, like this sparrow-hawk, have strong claws, sharp eyes and hooked beaks to help catch tiny animals hidden in the grass far beneath them.

▽ Birds often have dull feathers to help them hide among their surroundings. But some, like these male birds of paradise, are brightly coloured. This helps them to attract females.

blue bird of paradise

Raggiana bird of paradise

black-billed touraco

△ Many birds live on or near water. The jaçana has large feet and long claws, which help it to walk on floating leaves. Unlike most birds, it is the male jaçana that looks after the eggs, not the female.

rose-ringed parakeet

Find out more

Eagle
Ostrich, Emu and Cassowary
Parrot
Penguin

Eagle

Strong wings, sharp eyes and powerful talons make eagles great hunters. Their large, hooked bills are used for slicing open and eating – not for killing. They also scavenge if they find dead animals. These big birds of prey are found in regions from the cold Arctic to the warm tropics.

◁ The golden eagle (left) and the white-tailed sea eagle are the most widespread eagle species. They are found in Europe and northern Asia. Like most eagles, they nest on cliffs, raising one or two chicks a year.

△ The North American bald eagle is the national bird of the United States. It is not really bald, but has contrasting white head and brown body feathers. It lives close to lakes, rivers and coasts.

Fact box

• Because they are so strong, eagles have been symbols of war and national power for thousands of years.
• Eagles mate for life and return to use the same nest every year.

▷ Harpy eagles come from the jungles of South America and the South Pacific. They are powerful hunters, eating sloths, macaws and monkeys. The great harpy eagle (right) is the largest eagle.

Find out more
Bird
Owl
Vulture

Vulture

Vultures are large, strange-looking birds with wide wingspans. They are found worldwide – on mountains and plains, and in forests. They feed on rotting meat.

◁ Many species of vulture, like the king vulture (left), have no head or neck feathers. This keeps them clean when feeding. The king vulture's brightly coloured skin flaps are used in mating displays.

△ Many vulture species have incredible eyesight. They fly high in the air, looking for predators' kills.

▽ Vultures do a vital job because they clean up the carcasses left behind by predators. Once they spot a carcass, they glide down to feed. Some vultures have adapted to living in towns, and scavenge on rubbish dumps.

△ Vultures, like this white-backed vulture, often sit in the trees around a lion or hyena kill, waiting until the larger animals have had their fill.

Eurasian griffin

Ruppell's griffin

African white-backed vulture

lappet-faced vulture

Find out more
Bird
Eagle
Owl

Owl

Owls are birds of prey that hunt mainly at night. They use their sensitive hearing and large eyes (which give them good night vision) to catch animals such as mice and rabbits. Owls have soft feathers that allow them to fly silently. The hooting cry of some species is easy to recognize.

△ Tawny owls were once found only in woodlands. Today, they also live in towns and cities, where they hunt mice and rats. During the day, they settle in the trees of parks and gardens.

◁ The burrowing owls of North and South America live in burrows in the ground. They either dig a hole themselves or use one left by another animal, such as a gopher.

∇ Barn owls build nests in buildings, hollow trees or old hawk's nests. The round, flat shape of the barn owl's head helps it to hear its prey. Once it has caught the animal, the adult brings it to the chicks in the nest.

Fact box

• Owls can swivel their heads almost all the way round when they are listening for sounds.
• Snowy owls live in the Arctic. They mainly hunt lemmings. These owls nest on the ground.

Find out more
Bat
Bird
Eagle

Parrot

Parrots live in warm, tropical places around the world. They have strong, hooked beaks for cracking nuts and seeds. Each foot has two pairs of toes, which helps the birds to perch and to grip food.

▷ Macaws are brilliantly coloured parrots from South America. They are large, noisy birds and their piercing screams can often be heard in tropical rainforests.

△ Cockatoos are parrots found in Australia. This sulphur-crested cockatoo has a crest that it can raise and lower. Cockatoos are popular as pets, and often learn to copy human speech.

▷ Lovebirds are brightly coloured small parrots that live in Africa and Madagascar. They get their name from the way they sit together in pairs, resting their heads against each other.

Find out more
Bird
Hummingbird
Peacock
Toucan

Toucan

Toucans live in the tropical forests of the Americas. Their colourful beaks are thought to frighten off other birds. Although the beak is almost as big as the bird's body, it is very light. Toucans also have long tails to help them balance.

▽ Toucans gather in the treetops to roost and to feed on fruit. In order to swallow, they have to juggle their food in their beaks, then toss back their heads and catch it.

Fact box

• There are almost 40 species of toucan. The largest are up to 60cm long.
• The larger toucans sometimes eat eggs, small birds, frogs and lizards.
• Toucans are some of the noisiest birds in the forest. Their calls include loud croaks, barks and hoots.

▷ Bristles at the end of the toucan's long tongue act like a brush, helping it to hold on to its food.

◁ The hornbills of Africa, Asia and some Pacific islands also have large beaks. They get their name from the horny structure on top of their beaks, which are strong enough to crush small reptiles.

Find out more
Bird
Flamingo, Heron and Stork
Hummingbird

Gull

Gulls, or seagulls, are large, sturdy sea birds with webbed feet. There are over 40 species, found in coastal areas all over the world. Sometimes gulls are found inland, in the countryside and in towns and cities.

△ Gulls eat many different foods, including fish, eggs, earthworms and insects. They also scavenge for food on rubbish dumps.

▽ Baby gulls are covered in soft, fluffy feathers, called down. The chicks are fed by their parents until they have grown their flight feathers.

▽ Gulls are strong fliers, soaring and gliding on the strong sea breezes. Many gulls nest on cliffs, forming large and noisy colonies.

▽ Parents often have to fend off other gulls, like the lesser black-backed gull, that try to eat eggs and chicks from their nests.

Find out more
Albatross
Bird
Duck and Goose
Food
Puffin

Arctic tern

Arctic terns make the longest of all animal journeys. In autumn, after nesting on the Arctic coastline, these small sea birds fly south to spend a few months fishing on the other side of the world, in the Antarctic Ocean. In spring, they make the long trip north again to breed.

◁ Arctic terns lay two or three eggs in nests on the frozen Arctic ground, or tundra. They defend their eggs and chicks by diving at attacking predators.

△ The Arctic tern's round trip may be more than 36,000 kilometres. But, by being at each pole in summer, it spends nearly all its life in daylight. Chicks hatch in the northern summer, and by autumn they are ready to make the marathon flight south with their parents.

▽ Sooty and fairy terns are found on tropical islands. Unlike Arctic terns, they do not migrate.

sooty tern

fairy tern

Find out more
Albatross
Gull
Migration

Penguin

Penguins are sea birds that live in some of the world's coldest places. They are found on islands in the seas around Antarctica, and on the southern tips of South America, South Africa and Australia. Penguins cannot fly, but they can swim better than any other bird.

△ Penguins swim using their small, stiff wings like flippers. Their tails and feet are used for steering. They hunt fish and krill, a type of shrimp. Waterproof feathers and layers of fat keep them warm.

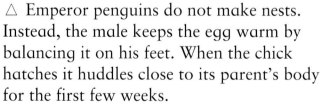

△ Emperor penguins do not make nests. Instead, the male keeps the egg warm by balancing it on his feet. When the chick hatches it huddles close to its parent's body for the first few weeks.

◁ The Adélie penguin of the Antarctic islands lives in big, noisy colonies. When calling to attract a mate or to warn off other penguins, they throw back their heads.

◁ While the emperor penguin (above) can be up to 120 centimetres tall, the smallest penguin is the fairy penguin, which reaches a height of just 40 centimetres.

Find out more
Baby animal
Ostrich, Emu and Cassowary
Seal and Sea lion

Puffin

Puffins are small sea birds that live in cold northern parts of the Atlantic and Pacific oceans. They have big beaks that become brightly coloured in the summer when they are looking for a mate. In winter the beak is dull yellow.

△ The tufted puffin of the North Pacific is one of only three puffin species in the world. The tuft is made up of long straw-coloured feathers that curve back from behind the bird's eyes.

△ Puffins live in large colonies on clifftops. They nest in long tunnels, which they either dig themselves or take over from rabbits. The females each lay a single egg here.

◁ Puffins feed mainly on sand eels, which they bring back to their nests in their beaks. Although they have a stumpy shape, puffins are fast fliers and swim under-water to catch the eels.

Find out more
Arctic tern
Bird
Duck and Goose
Gull
Penguin

Chicken and Turkey

Chickens and turkeys are kept as farm animals all over the world. They are related to wild birds that were tamed by humans over 4,000 years ago. Chickens and turkeys can fly for short distances, but they prefer to walk or run.

△ Farmyard chickens eat seeds and small insects. They will also peck grain that is sprinkled on the ground. On some big farms, however, hens are fed on special food and kept in small cages.

△ Male chickens are called cockerels and have large crests on their heads and a ruff of long feathers round their necks. They often make a loud crow, especially at daybreak. Female chickens are called hens. They are smaller and less colourful than cockerels. Hens are kept for both their meat and their eggs.

◁ Turkeys are big birds with a fleshy red 'wattle' round their necks. They come from North and Central America, and were first brought to Europe in about 1519 by Spanish explorers.

Find out more
Bird
Duck and Goose
Peacock
Pigeon and Dove
Swan

Duck and Goose

Ducks and geese are water birds. Members of this family live in most parts of the world. They have thick plumage (feathers) to keep them warm, and webbed feet for paddling along in water.

△ Geese are generally bigger than ducks and have longer necks. Geese have big beaks for pulling up and eating grass. Ducks have flatter beaks for sifting food from the water.

◁ Ducks have short legs and they waddle when they walk. Their feet have three front toes in a web and a rear toe that is separate. Almost all duck species live in fresh water. As well as feeding on insects and worms, they eat vegetable matter.

△ Eider ducks breed along icy northern coasts. To keep her eggs warm, the female lines the nest with fluffy feathers (down) plucked from her breast.

▽ Most Canada geese that breed in Canada and Alaska migrate to Mexico and the southern United States in winter. When they fly, they often make a loud honking noise.

△ Male ducks are called drakes. They often have colourful plumage, which is designed to attract females. Female ducks are usually dull brown.

Find out more
Bird
Gull
Migration
Swan

Swan

The swan is one of the world's largest water birds, with a wingspan of up to three metres. It has webbed feet for swimming and a wide beak for eating underwater plants. Swans guard their eggs closely and will fiercely attack humans if they feel threatened.

trumpeter swan

△ Swans in the Northern Hemisphere are white. Most are named after their calls, such as the trumpeter, whistling and whooper swans. The whistling swan migrates from the Canadian Arctic to spend the winter in the southern United States.

▽ Southern swans include the Australian black swan and the South American black-necked swan.

Australian black swan

Fact box
• Swans live for 20 years or more.
• Swans swallow stones to help their digestion. But many have accidentally eaten anglers' lead weights and been poisoned by them.
• Swans build a big nest that can float on the water.

△ Swans mate when they are five years old and the pairs remain loyal for life. Young swans, called cygnets, have fluffy grey feathers and short necks that make them look more like scruffy ducks. Their long necks and white plumage grow when they are a year old.

Find out more
Baby animal
Bird
Duck and Goose
Migration

Pigeon and Dove

Pigeons live in towns, woods and grasslands, in all parts of the world except for very cold places. They range from the dull grey pigeons seen in cities to the brightly coloured birds of the tropics. Small pigeons are called doves.

△ The rock dove was first tamed about 5,000 years ago in the Middle East. Wild rock doves still live in remote areas of Europe. The street pigeon found in towns and cities is descended from the wild rock dove.

Fact box

• The most famous extinct bird is the dodo – a big pigeon that once lived on Mauritius.
• New Guinea's crowned pigeons are turkey-sized.
• White doves are a symbol of peace. Pictures usually show them carrying an olive branch.

◁ Pigeons can find their way home over long distances. This is why homing pigeons have been used since ancient times to carry messages. In AD 1150 a pigeon post service was set up by the sultan of Baghdad. Today people hold races to see whose pigeon gets home fastest. Races can be over thousands of kilometres.

▽ Most pigeons, like this wood pigeon, build untidy nests in trees, where the female lays one or two eggs. Pigeons in towns nest on ledges on the sides of buildings.

Find out more
Arctic tern
Bird
Conservation
Owl

Swift and Swallow

Swifts and swallows are among the fastest and most agile in the air of all birds. They are able to fly non-stop for hours on end. Swifts have longer wings and fly higher than swallows. They hardly ever touch the ground. Swallows fly lower and sometimes rest on wires, roofs and trees.

△ Swifts are well adapted to constant flight. In fact, a swift is stranded if it lands on the ground, because its wings are too long and its legs are too short for it to take off.

△ A pair of swallows works together to build a mud nest, often under the roofs of houses. They bring insects to their hungry young.

Fact box
• Although the swift and the swallow look alike, they are not related.
• Swifts can fly at 70km/h.
• Tree swallows nest in holes in hollow trees.
• Swifts and swallows are found in all parts of the world.

▽ Swallows and swifts, like this Alpine swift, catch insects in flight at high speed. Bristles around their beaks guide the prey into their large mouths.

▷ In late summer, after they have raised their young, swallows migrate south to escape the cold winters and to search for food. Some birds that breed in Europe fly all the way to southern Africa. They return in summer each year to the same nest sites.

Europe

Africa

Find out more
Arctic tern
Bird
Migration
Reproduction

Hummingbird

When hummingbirds hover, their wings beat so fast that they hum, and this gives them their name. These tiny birds live in warm places in North and South America.

▽ Hummingbirds use their long beaks to reach the nectar deep inside flowers.

◁ Hummingbirds use up so much energy beating their wings that they need to feed often. The nectar they eat is full of sugar, which gives them energy quickly.

△ A hummingbird's wings swivel. This means it can hover near a flower while keeping its head perfectly still. It can also fly backwards.

Fact box

• Ruby-throated hummingbirds fly 800km nonstop across the Gulf of Mexico when migrating.
• Hummingbirds normally lay two eggs, which are the smallest of any bird.
• There are over 300 species of hummingbird.

▷ All hummingbirds are tiny, but the bee hummingbird of Cuba is the world's smallest bird. It is just 5.5 centimetres long – no bigger than a child's thumb.

Find out more
Bird
Migration
Ostrich
Reproduction

Flamingo, Heron and Stork

Flamingos live in colonies on shallow lakes in Africa, South America and Asia. They are pink with large wings, slim necks and long, thin legs for wading in water. The largest is the great flamingo which is 1.5 metres tall. Flamingos, herons and storks are all in the same group of birds.

▽ Herons are long legged like flamingos. They wade along the edges of lakes and rivers, hunting for fish. When they spot one, they spear it with their sharp beak. Like most wading birds, they often stand on one leg. They tuck the other under the body to keep warm.

▽ Storks are also wading birds. White storks spend the winter in Africa and in summer fly to Europe to breed. Many Europeans think storks bring good luck. They build platforms on their chimneys so the birds can make their nests on them.

△ Flamingos wade through the shallows moving their heads from side to side. Their specially shaped beaks act like sieves, filtering shrimps and other tiny animals from the muddy water. Flamingos get their pink colour from the shrimps they eat.

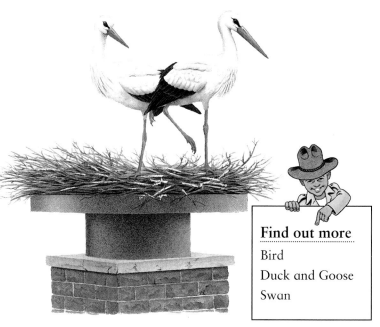

Find out more
Bird
Duck and Goose
Swan

Peacock

The peacock is one of the world's most beautiful birds. Peacocks first lived in Asia but, because of their colourful feathers, they have been kept in parks and gardens all over the world for thousands of years. They have a loud piercing cry and eat snails, frogs, insects and plants.

▽ Peacocks have shiny green or blue tail feathers, tipped with a pattern like an eye. To attract females, they raise their tails and vibrate them.

▽ The female is called a peahen. Peahens have short tails, and much duller feathers than the males.

Fact box

• Peacocks have the longest tail feathers of any bird – over 1.5m.
• In 1936, a hunt started for the African Congo peacock when a single feather was discovered. The bird itself was finally found 23 years later.

▽ Pheasants are members of the same family as peacocks. Male pheasants also have long, decorative tails and brightly patterned feathers. Pheasants originally came from the Far East, but have been bred in many countries for hunting.

Find out more

Bird

Chicken and Turkey

Kiwi

Kiwis are birds that live in the thick forests of New Zealand. Many of these forests are being cut down, so kiwis are now quite rare. Kiwis have a long beak, short legs and no tail. Their wings are too small for flying and are hidden under a coat of long, fine feathers.

Fact box
- Kiwis are the size of chickens and weigh about 4kg.
- A kiwi egg weighs about 450g and is nine times as big as a hen's egg.
- Kiwis are related to the giant moa, which is now extinct.

△ Kiwis mainly come out at night. In the daytime, they sleep in burrows in the earth. Kiwis can run very fast if threatened, and defend themselves with their claws.

△ Birds can usually see well, but the kiwi's eyesight is weak. However, unlike most birds, the kiwi has a very good sense of smell, and this helps it to find food. Its nostrils are at the tip of the beak, and the kiwi uses it to search the ground for worms, insects, seeds and berries.

▷ The kakapo also comes from New Zealand. Like the kiwi, it cannot fly, so it is easily caught by pet cats and dogs. It is now one of the world's rarest birds.

Find out more
Bird
Ostrich
Parrot
Penguin

Ostrich, Emu and Cassowary

Not all birds can fly. Although they have small wings, the world's biggest birds – ostriches, cassowaries and emus – can only walk and run.

▽ Emus are the second tallest birds, growing to 1.8 metres. They live on the grasslands of Australia.

△ Ostriches lay up to eight giant eggs in a nest on the ground. The male sits on the eggs at night; the female, during the day.

▽ Male ostriches are black and white. They are the biggest birds of all – often 2.5 metres tall. Females are slightly smaller and greyish-brown. They can run at 65 kilometres per hour.

Fact box

• Ostriches live in Africa.
• Ostrich eggs are the biggest of all bird eggs.

◁ Cassowaries live in the forests of New Guinea and Australia. They are 1.5 metres tall and have featherless heads with a bony helmet on the top. If attacked, they will kick and slash with their clawed feet. Their middle toe is as sharp as a dagger.

Find out more
Bird
Kiwi

Reptiles

and

Amphibians

Reptile

Reptiles are animals with scaly skin. Some species live on land, others live in water. There are many different kinds of reptile, including turtles, snakes and crocodiles. They live in the warmer parts of the world.

△ Although some snakes are dangerous to humans, many are harmless and can be kept as pets. Their skin feels dry and not slimy, as some people expect.

△ To make your own reptile collage, draw the shape of a lizard on a piece of card. Using different-coloured lentils, glue the 'scales' on in stripes.

▷ Reptiles cannot control their own body temperature. To get warm, these lizards must sit in the sun. To cool down, they have to move to the shade.

▽ Some reptiles have tongues that act like noses. Instead of sniffing the air to pick up a scent, they stick out their tongues and 'taste' it. This helps them to find their prey.

△ Most reptiles lay eggs. While the shells of turtle and crocodile eggs are hard, snake and lizard eggs are soft and leathery.

Find out more

Alligator and Crocodile

Komodo dragon and Iguana

Lizard

Rattlesnake

Turtle and Tortoise

Chameleon

Chameleons are unusual lizards that can change their skin colour. They do this when they are angry or frightened, when the light or temperature levels change, or to hide themselves.

△ There are special cells called melanophores underneath a chameleon's skin. These give the chameleon its ability to change colour, which helps make it difficult to see.

▽ A chameleon will sit in a tree waiting to catch insects. A strong, curled tail holds it to the branch, while swivelling eyes allow it to see prey in two directions at the same time. Then its long tongue darts out to catch the prey.

Fact box

• There are about 100 species of chameleon.
• Around 50 of these species live on the island of Madagascar.
• Most species of chameleon live in trees, but come down to lay their eggs in the soil.

▷ The Madagascan pygmy chameleon is the smallest species at about 2.5 centimetres long. It lives mainly on leaves on the forest floor. Most chameleons are between 17 and 25 centimetres long, but some can grow up to 60 centimetres. While most chameleons eat insects, the bigger ones also eat birds.

Find out more

Alligator and Crocodile

Cobra

Lizard

Reptile

Lizard

Lizards are reptiles. They have scaly skin, long tails and usually live in warm countries. Although they can dart about very quickly, they are cold-blooded and need to lie in the sun to keep warm.

△ The Gila monster is a lizard that lives in the North American deserts. Bright red and black markings warn that it has a poisonous bite.

△ Many lizards turn darker when basking in the sun. This helps their bodies to absorb its heat better.

△ The Australian thorny devil looks frightening, but it is harmless. Its sharp spines save it from being eaten by predators.

Fact box

• The smallest lizards, the geckos of the Virgin Islands, are 35 millimetres long.
• If some species of lizard are caught by the tail, the tail breaks off. A new one will grow in its place within eight months.

◁ The frilled lizard of Australia lifts up its huge neck collar to scare off attackers.

Find out more

Chameleon
Komodo dragon and Iguana
Reptile

Komodo dragon and Iguana

Komodo dragons are not really dragons and do not breathe fire. But they are three metres long – the biggest lizards alive. They mainly live on the Indonesian island of Komodo.

△ Iguanas, like this common iguana, are also big lizards, but they are smaller than Komodo dragons and live in North and South America. Common iguanas can grow up to 1.8 metres in length, and may have spines running along their backs.

◁ Komodo dragons eat carrion (rotting meat) and also hunt deer and wild pigs. They use their long, forked tongues to pick up the scent of their prey. They attack the animal with a short, fast sprint, and use their powerful jaws to rip it to pieces. Komodo dragons sometimes live to be 100 years old.

◁ The marine iguanas of the Galapagos Islands in the Pacific Ocean spend most of their lives beside the sea. They feed on the seaweed and algae that grow below the water line, and can eat underwater for up to 20 minutes.

Find out more
Chameleon
Lizard
Reptile

Cobra

Cobras are poisonous snakes found in Africa, India and Asia. The most deadly cobras are the mambas of Africa. A bite from a mamba will kill unless the victim is given antivenin (an antidote to snake venom) very quickly. Many people die each year from cobra bites.

Fact box

• Cobras eat small vertebrates (creatures with backbones).
• The black mamba moves as fast as a running human.
• Cobra venom stops the heart and lungs from working.

△ The king cobra is found in areas stretching from southern China to Indonesia. Reaching 5.5 metres in length, it is the world's longest poisonous snake. The female king cobra lays up to 40 eggs.

▷ In India, snake charmers catch common cobras. They play a tune on a pipe and the cobra rises up from the basket to 'dance'.

▽ One of the cobra's main predators is the mongoose. Mongooses move very quickly and can avoid getting bitten. When frightened, the cobra rears up and spreads its hood.

Find out more

Lizard
Rattlesnake
Reptile

Rattlesnake

Rattlesnakes are found in North and South America. They are named after their spooky rattle, which warns other animals that they are very poisonous. There are about 30 species of rattlesnake.

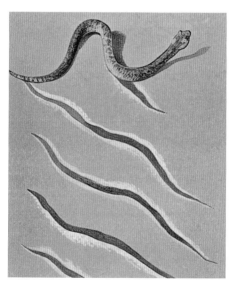

◁ The sidewinder is a rattlesnake that lives in sandy deserts in Mexico and the southwestern United States. Its unusual method of moving sideways leaves a distinctive trail.

△ Most rattlesnakes rest during the day and hunt small rodents at night. They detect prey by 'tasting' the air for smells with their forked tongue. As the prey moves closer the rattlesnake feels its body warmth with heat-sensitive pits on the sides of its face.

▷ Inside a rattlesnake's tail is a set of hard, loose pieces. It is these that produce the rattling noise. You can make your own rattle by threading some bottle tops onto a long nail and attaching it to a length of wood (get an adult to help you). You might scare a few people!

Fact box

• At 2.5m long, the eastern diamondback is the biggest rattlesnake.
• A rattlesnake's poison comes out of two fangs in its upper jaw.
• The bite of a rattlesnake can be deadly.

Find out more

Cobra
Communication
Defence
Habitat
Reptile

Alligator and Crocodile

Alligators and crocodiles are large reptiles that live in rivers and swamps in tropical areas. They float beneath the surface of the water, with only their eyes and nostrils showing, ready to snap up fish, turtles, and even big mammals in their huge jaws.

△ Crocodiles are cold-blooded creatures that spend much of their lives in the water, keeping cool and hunting. The rest of their time is spent on the riverbank, soaking up the sun's rays. This helps to give them energy.

◁▽ The American alligator (left) has a broader and shorter jaw than the crocodile (below). Both alligators and crocodiles have between 60 and 80 teeth in their powerful jaws. They use the teeth to rip their prey to pieces.

Fact box

• Crocodiles have existed for over 200 million years.
• Alligators can grow up to six metres long.
• The largest, crocodile, the saltwater, grows to almost eight metres.

▽ Alligators and crocodiles lay up to 90 eggs in a nest on the riverbank made from mud and leaves. When the young hatch, they call to their mother. She digs them out, picks them up gently in her mouth, and carries them down to the water.

Find out more
Komodo dragon and Iguana
Lizard

Turtle and Tortoise

Turtles and tortoises are reptiles that live in warm climates. Turtles are found in water; tortoises are slow land animals. The soft bodies of both animals are protected by a heavy shell.

△ Many turtles spend nearly all their lives in the sea. Their legs are shaped like paddles, which helps them to swim. Only females ever come onto land. They do this to lay eggs – on the same beach as they were born.

◁ Tortoises are found in Africa, Asia, Europe, and North and South America. They grow slowly and can live to be more than 150 years old.

◁ **1** The female turtle crawls out of the sea to lay her eggs. **2** She buries them in a hole, then returns to the water. The sun's heat keeps them warm until they are ready to hatch.

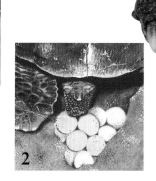

▷ **3** Left on their own, the tiny babies must break free of their eggs and dig their way out of the hole. **4** They must hurry to the sea before they are eaten by other animals.

Find out more
Chameleon
Lizard
Reptile
Reproduction

Amphibian

Amphibians are animals that live both in the water and on the land. Frogs, toads, newts and caecilians are all amphibians. They are found everywhere except Antarctica, particularly in warm places.

△ Newts have long tails and four short legs, and they look like lizards. However, they do not have scales and their skin is moist.

△ Adult frogs and toads have four legs and no tail. Some frogs inflate their throats to make a loud croak. This helps them to attract a mate.

▷ Caecilians have no legs and resemble worms. They live underground in tropical places. Unlike most amphibians, the female caecilian guards her eggs.

◁ **1** A home-made mini-pond is a great way of attracting frogs and newts to your garden. You will need a washing-up bowl, some sand, pondweed, and a few stones and rocks.

◁ **2** Dig a hole in a corner of your garden and drop the bowl into it. Cover the bottom with the sand and stones, making sure that some of the rocks rise above the surface of the water. Add the pondweed, then fill the bowl with water. Over the next few weeks, watch to see if your pond has any visitors.

Find out more
Fish
Frog and Toad
Lizard
Reproduction
Worm

Frog and Toad

Frogs and toads are amphibians so they live both in water and on land. Frogs have moist skins but toads are normally dry. While frogs use their strong back legs for jumping, toads walk. Both animals are good swimmers.

△ The female Surinam toad has special pockets on her back in which her eggs grow. After 80 days, the young toads emerge from the pockets.

△ Many tropical frogs are brightly coloured. This warns other animals that they are poisonous. The poison of the South American poison dart frog (bottom) is so strong that native people put it on the tips of their arrows.

▷ **1** Most frogs and toads lay their eggs, called spawn, in water. **2** After two weeks, tadpoles hatch. **3** Like fish, they breathe through gills, but gradually grow legs. **4** After three months, the gills shrink, the tail gets short and the lungs develop. **5, 6** The tiny frogs are able to leave the water and grow into adults on land.

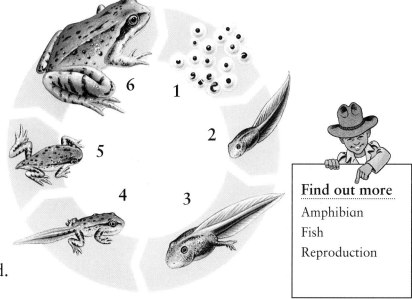

Find out more

Amphibian
Fish
Reproduction

Fish

Fish

Fish live in saltwater and freshwater all over the world. They come in many different shapes and sizes, but most are covered in scales and have strong fins for swimming.

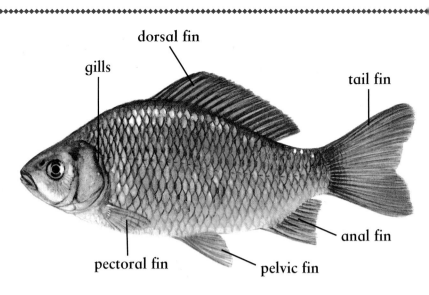

gills

dorsal fin

tail fin

anal fin

pelvic fin

pectoral fin

◁ Like us, fish need oxygen to live. But instead of breathing air, they absorb the oxygen in water. Water enters the mouth and is swept over the gills. The oxygen passes from the water into tiny blood vessels in the gills.

water out

water in

▽ Fish often swim in groups called shoals. One reason they do this is for protection. Many fish together can confuse a predator, making it hard for it to single out a fish to attack.

▽ **1** A fish's scales all lie in the same direction to help the fish slip through water. You can see how scales work by sticking strips of paper in layers onto a fish outline. (Start from the tail end.)

1

2

△ **2** Now run your hand over the paper scales from head to tail, and then from tail to head. It should feel very different.

Find out more
Flatfish
Salmon and Trout
Shark

Goldfish and Carp

Goldfish and carp originally came from lakes and streams in Asia and were first brought to Europe by the Romans. Goldfish are often small and brightly coloured; carp are larger and usually have plainer colouring.

common goldfish

comet

△ Goldfish survive well in both outdoor ponds and tanks indoors. They come in a wide range of colours and shapes.

silver carp

△ **1** Looking after goldfish is easy. You will need a tank with clean gravel and a few large objects. You should also put in a filter to help keep the water clean.

▷ **2** Fill the tank with water that is at room temperature and carefully place the goldfish in the tank. You will need to feed them daily and you must be sure to clean the tank and partly change the water regularly.

△ Carp can now be found in North America as well as Europe. Grass carp are helpful to humans because they eat pondweed. In China, the silver carp is bred for food.

Find out more
Fish
Flatfish
Food
Salmon and Trout

Salmon and Trout

Salmon and some kinds of trout are found in the cold northern parts of the Atlantic and Pacific Oceans. Most types of trout, however, live in fresh water. Large salmon can weigh up to 30 kilograms, while the largest trout weigh over 13.5 kilograms.

△ There are many different types of trout. The brightly coloured rainbow trout (above) is one of the most common. It was introduced to Europe from North America and people often catch it for sport.

▷ Before they breed, salmon migrate thousands of kilometres from their homes in the sea, back to the rivers where they were born. They battle upstream against strong currents, clearing obstacles such as waterfalls by leaping up to 3.5 metres high.

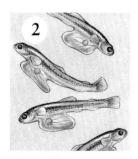

▽ **3** After a year the young salmon develop red stripes on their sides.
4 By the time they are 15 centimetres long, the salmon are silver coloured. They are now ready to journey down the river to the sea, where they will grow into adults and repeat the cycle.

△ **1** The female salmon makes a small hole in the gravel on the riverbed and lays her eggs. The male then fertilizes them. **2** At birth, young salmon have a pouch on their sides that contains food.

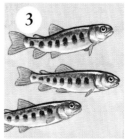

Find out more
Fish
Goldfish and Carp
Migration
Reproduction

Flatfish

Flatfish are found in all of the world's oceans and seas. They range in weight and size from the huge Atlantic halibut to the small species of sole. They nestle on the seabed waiting for their favourite food – shellfish or smaller fish.

▽ Anglerfish are flatfish that live on the seabed. They are covered in lumps and flaps that act as camouflage as they lie in wait among the seaweed and rocks. Like fishermen, they lure their prey with the rod on their nose, and as soon as it is close, the small fish is snapped up.

△ Like all flatfish, the plaice family are coloured on their upper side and white on their underside. Plaice have their eyes on the upper side of their heads.

△ Young flatfish are born with an eye on either side of the head. As they grow, one eye moves to the same side of the head as the other eye. Meanwhile, the body and skull flatten out, and the mouth moves to the same side as the eyes.

Find out more

Camouflage
Fish
Food
Shellfish

Seahorse

Seahorses are fish that live in warm seas. Because they swim upright and are covered by bony armour, they do not look like fish. However, they are related to the stickleback.

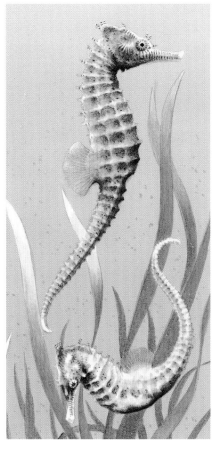

△ Seahorses spend much of their lives anchored by their tails to seaweed. They feed on shrimps and plankton, which they suck into their long mouths.

▷ When seahorses mate, the male and female meet belly to belly and the female lays her eggs in a pouch on the male. Five weeks later, up to 200 young hatch from the male's body, looking just like tiny adults.

◁ The sea dragon is a type of seahorse that is found around the Australian coastline. It is 1.5 metres long and camouflaged by leafy-looking growths all over its body.

Find out more
Camouflage
Fish
Reproduction
Shrimp and Prawn

Shark

Sharks are the most fearsome predators in the ocean. They are excellent hunters and find their prey either by its smell, or by tracking the tiny electrical currents that the prey's body gives out.

great white shark

△ The world's most dangerous shark is the great white. It can grow to be 12 metres long, and has a huge mouth full of sharp, pointed teeth. Great whites are found in warm waters all over the world. They sometimes attack bathers and surfers, but seals and sea lions are their favourite prey.

hammerhead shark

◁ The hammerhead shark uses its huge head to steer itself. Sharks are a kind of fish, but instead of fish scales they have rough skin, and instead of bone their skeleton is made of rubbery cartilage.

◁ At over 15 metres long, the whale shark is the largest of all fish. It feeds on some of the smallest creatures in the sea – plankton.

Find out more
Dolphin
Fish
Killer whale
Seal and Sea lion

Invertebrates

Worm

Worms are soft-bodied animals with no backbone or legs. Some, like the earthworm, live in the soil. Others live in the sea. Worms can even live on – or even inside – other animals.

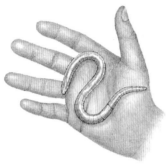

◁ Hold an earthworm in your hand and you will see the segments of its body. It squeezes and stretches these to move along.

▽ Earthworms bore their way through soil by eating it. Soil goes in the front end of the worm and comes out the back. Piles of softened soil are called worm-casts.

△ Try making your own worm farm. Put alternate layers of moist soil and sand into a large glass jar. Place some worms on the top, with leaves for them to eat, then cover the jar with net secured with an elastic band. Wrap black paper around the jar. After a couple of days, take off the paper and see what the worms have done to the layers and leaves. Release the worms back into the wild after a week or so.

worm-cast

insect grub

coiled worm

Find out more
Ant and Termite
Badger
Food
Reproduction
Slug and Snail

Slug and Snail

Slugs and snails are found all over the world, both on land and in water. They have feelers on their heads, soft bodies, and a single muscular foot that is also their stomach. Snails have shells to protect them but slugs do not.

◁ Watch how slugs and snails move by placing them on a piece of clear glass or plastic. You will see that they ooze a trail of slime to ease them along their way.

△ Garden slugs and snails mostly feed on rotting plants. But they sometimes eat growing plants, so they can be bad for gardens. Their mouths are full of tiny teeth.

▽ Snails are known for moving slowly, but a snail race can still be very exciting. On a board, make three lanes with string held in place by pins. Chalk a line at the start and at the finish, then start them racing. First past the finish is the winner.

Fact box

• Land species have lungs to breathe; water species have gills.
• The giant land snail can be 30cm long.
• Tropical cone snails feed on fish. First they paralyze them by injecting nerve poison from a tooth on the end of their tongues.

Find out more
Defence
Fish
Habitat
Peacock
Shellfish
Worm

Jellyfish

Jellyfish are sea creatures whose soft, wobbly bodies are made almost entirely of water. The smallest jellyfish are just a few centimetres in width, and the largest can measure more than two metres across.

▽ The Australian box jellyfish stuns its prey with its poisonous tentacles. Then it pulls the creature towards its mouth, inside its bell-shaped body.

▽ The Portuguese man-of-war has a bag filled with gas on top of its body. As it floats above the water, the man-of-war trails its tentacles behind it. These tentacles can be up to 50 metres long and are a danger to swimmers as well as fish.

Fact box

• Many humans have been killed by the sting of the Australian box jellyfish.

• Jellyfish are invertebrates. This means that they have no spine (backbone).

• The largest jellyfish measured had tentacles 36.5m long.

△ Some types of jellyfish drift along wherever the ocean currents carry them. But others can propel themselves rapidly by pumping water out from folds in their bodies.

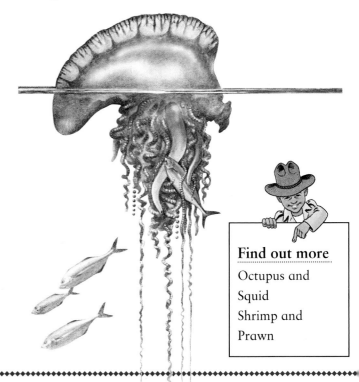

Find out more
Octupus and Squid
Shrimp and Prawn

128

Octopus and Squid

The octopus is a sea creature with eight long arms called tentacles. These can wind round objects and have suckers on them that grip. The squid is related to the octopus, but it has ten arms.

◁ Squid range in length from 1.5 centimetres up to 20 metres for the largest species. Two of their ten arms are especially long and have suckers on the end.

△ Octopuses can be up to 5.4 metres long and have an arm span of nine metres. They live in caves on the sea bed. When they leave the caves, they may be attacked by sharks or moray eels – like the one seen here. If octopuses are in danger they squirt out thick black ink, which hides them while they escape. They either 'walk' over the sea floor or they push themselves forward using a jet of water shot out of a hole in their bodies.

◁ Octopuses ambush their prey, such as crabs, shellfish and shrimps. Their tentacles draw the victim towards their powerful, birdlike beak. This is hidden at the base of the tentacles.

Find out more
Crab
Food
Shellfish
Shrimp and
Prawn

Shellfish

Shellfish are water creatures whose soft bodies are protected by hard shells. Like slugs, snails and octopuses, shellfish are molluscs. They are found in freshwater and saltwater all over the world.

△ When shellfish die, all that remains is the shell. If you go to the seaside, collect as many different shells as you can. Later, you can display them on a board with their names underneath them.

Fact box
• Some shellfish have just one shell, others have a pair.
• Shells are made from minerals. These make the shells very hard.
• Shellfish have existed on Earth for 600 million years.

◁ Most shellfish feed by filtering tiny food particles from the water. Some shellfish stay on the same rock all their lives. They anchor themselves with a single sucker foot, or by threads.

▽ Mussels have two matching shells that clamp shut when they are in danger. They hold on to rocks using threads that are so strong they can resist huge storm waves.

lambis shell   **top shell**

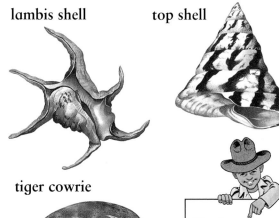

tiger cowrie

Find out more
Crab

Octopus and Squid

Shrimp and Prawn

Shrimps and prawns live in seas, rivers and lakes almost everywhere. They are related to lobsters but are smaller and are better swimmers. Prawns are slightly bigger than shrimps.

△ The pistol shrimp, which grows to about four centimetres long, has very large claws. It snaps them together to stun its prey.

▽ **1** Make an underwater viewer to look at shrimps and prawns in rock pools. Get an adult to cut the bottom off a clear plastic bottle. Stretch cling film over the cut end and secure with an elastic band.

▽ **2** You will need to keep still, as these animals are easily frightened.

◁ Shrimps and prawns often search for food on the seabed. They eat small plants and animals. They swim by flicking their fan-like tails.

Norway lobster

ghost shrimp

female common prawn

male common prawn

common shrimp

Find out more

Crab
Octopus and
Squid
Shellfish

Crab

Crabs are creatures with ten legs and a hard shell. Most live in the sea or along the shore, where they scurry sideways. Their two front legs are frightening pincers, used for feeding and fighting off attackers.

△ Hermit crabs do not have their own shells, but live in the empty shells of sea snails and whelks. As a hermit crab grows, it moves into bigger shells.

▽ Tropical horseshoe crabs are a very ancient species, related to spiders and scorpions. They emerge from the sea in large numbers to lay eggs on the shore.

◁ The legs of some crabs are adapted for swimming. The back legs of this swimmer crab are flattened like tiny paddles.

▷ Fiddler crabs live in muddy mangrove swamps in all regions of the world. One of the male fiddler crab's claws is huge. He waves it to attract females to his burrow.

Find out more
Defence
Shellfish
Spider

Spider

Spiders belong to the class of animals called arachnids. They feed mainly on insects. Most spiders have large, hairy, round abdomens (rear body parts) and eight legs. All spiders make silk and many spin webs.

◁ The female black widow spider is one of the few spiders with venom (poison) harmful to humans. Most people bitten by it recover fully.

Fact box
• The goliath bird-eating spider is the biggest spider in the world. It is large enough to cover a dinner plate.
• Tropical orb-web spiders build some of the largest webs, at nearly two metres across.

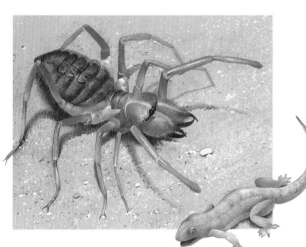

△ Camel spiders live in deserts in Africa and Asia. They do not spin webs, but pounce on their prey and crush them in their strong jaws. They feed on scorpions, birds and small lizards.

▷ Many spiders spin webs of sticky silk to catch their prey. Silk is very strong and it is also stretchy. Here, a garden spider wraps a fly in its silk, then stuns it with venom from its fangs.

◁ Spiders live in many places, from hot deserts to cold mountains, from mountains to lakes. Some spiders that live near water eat small fish.

Find out more
Fly
Insect
Lizard

Insect

There are more insects on Earth than any other group of creatures. There are probably more than a million species and they live in almost every region and habitat in the world.

◁ Insects can carry out complicated tasks and will often build elaborate structures. The potter wasp, for example, builds her nest out of chewed-up wood or mud. She kills caterpillars and brings them back as food for her young.

Fact box
• The smallest insect is the fairy fly, which is just 0.2mm long.
• Mayflies live just a few hours, but some beetles live many years.
• An ant can lift 50 times its own weight.
• The largest cockroaches are about 10cm long.

▷ All insects have six legs, a pair of antennae and a body made of three parts: the head, the thorax and the abdomen. The legs are attached to the thorax. Insects are invertebrates, so instead of having bones the body is encased in a tough shell. Many insects also have two pairs of wings.

antenna

thorax

head

leg

abdomen

◁ Many insects only come out at night. A good way to watch them on a summer evening is to hang a white sheet on a washing line and to shine a torch at it. Moths and other flying insects will be attracted to the patch of light.

Find out more
Ant and Termite
Bee and Wasp
Beetle
Butterfly and Moth
Fly

Ant and Termite

Ants and termites live in enormous nests called colonies. Inside most nests there is a queen who lays eggs, and thousands of workers who run the colony and feed her. Each worker has a job to do – some act as soldiers guarding the nest, others collect food, and cleaners keep it tidy.

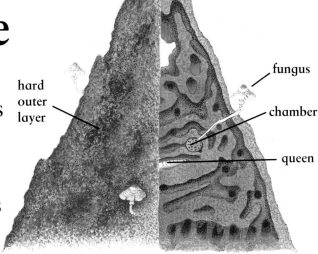
hard outer layer

fungus

chamber

queen

△ In grassland areas, termites build castles of mud that are seven metres tall. Most termites feed on plants, but some live off a fungus that grows in their nests.

▽ A fungus grows in the nests of leafcutter ants. The ants take bits of leaf to the fungus, which 'eats' the leaf and gives off sugars for the ants to eat.

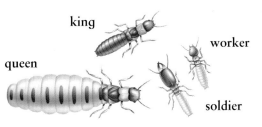
king

queen

worker

soldier

◁ The queen of a termite nest lays 30,000 eggs a day. She can be 11 centimetres long. The king can grow to two centimetres, and the soldiers and workers are about half as big.

▷ Army ants march in vast swarms that can be 12 metres wide. They prey on insects and small animals. Worker ants take prey back to the nest while soldier ants stand guard. Ants have harder bodies and smaller waists than termites, which are sometimes called white ants.

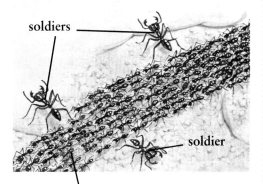
soldiers

soldier

workers

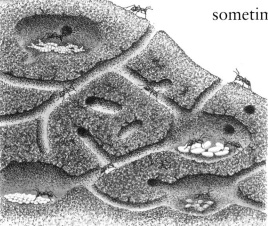

◁ Although not as tall as a termite's nest, there are lots of compartments inside an ant's nest. This is where eggs are laid and where young ants are cared for. Food is stored here too.

Find out more
Aardvark
Bee and Wasp
Insect
Reproduction

Fly

There are many types of fly, and they are found everywhere. Unlike other insects, they have just one pair of wings for flying; their tiny back wings are only used for balance. A few flies carry deadly diseases, but many help plants by carrying pollen from one flower to another.

△ The African tsetse fly (pronounced 'tetsy') carries a disease called sleeping sickness. It spreads the disease from wild animals to humans and livestock by biting them and drinking their blood.

Fact box

• House-flies beat their wings 200 times a second.
• Midges beat their wings 1,000 times a second. It is this which makes the buzzing sound common to all flies.

△ The hover-fly, also called the flower-fly, gets its name from the fact that it hovers round flowers. Hover-flies have markings like wasps.

▽ Like all flies, dung-flies spend the first part of their lives as maggots. During this time, they live inside the dung left by animals. They feed on the dung and, in doing so, clear it up.

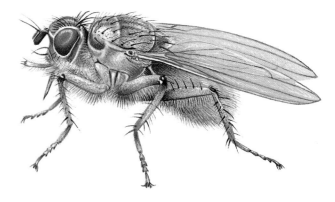

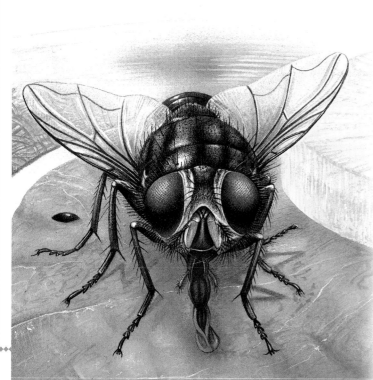

◁ Bluebottles (left) and house-flies feed on all kinds of food. They have 'taste buds' on their feet. These tell them whether something they have landed on is good to eat.

Find out more
Ant and Termite
Bee and Wasp
Beetle
Insect

Bee and Wasp

Bees and wasps are easy insects to spot because of their black and yellow, or black and white, striped bodies. Wasps and worker bees have a stinging tail. Bees only sting in self-defence and usually die afterwards.

▽ Honeybees are ruled by a queen. They build wax rooms, called cells. **1** The queen lays an egg in each cell. **2** This grows into a larva. **3, 4** The worker bees feed it. **5, 6** Soon it grows into an adult and emerges.

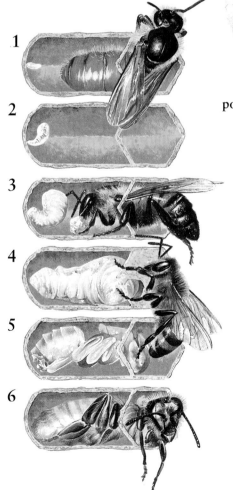

1

2

3

4

5

6

pollen sac

△ Bees collect the sweet juice, or nectar, from flowers and use it to make honey. They keep the honey in cells to feed their growing young.

◁ The bumblebee is larger and more furry than the honeybee. It collects pollen from flowers using its hindlegs. The bee carries the pollen in pollen sacs. Flowers need bees to spread pollen in order to reproduce.

▽ Wasps are different from bees because they feed their young on insects, not honey. They use their sting to kill the insects. Adult wasps eat the sugars found in fruit, and so are attracted by the smell of sweet food or liquids.

Find out more
Fly
Insect
Reproduction

137

Butterfly and Moth

These flying insects are found worldwide, especially in warm places. Most butterflies are colourful and fly by day. Moths usually fly at night and are dull in colour.

△ Swallowtail butterflies are so-called because their wings look like the tails of swallows.

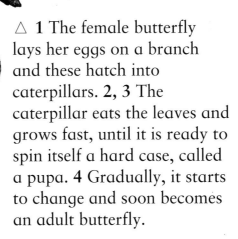

1 egg

2 caterpillar

3 pupa

4 adult

△ **1** The female butterfly lays her eggs on a branch and these hatch into caterpillars. **2, 3** The caterpillar eats the leaves and grows fast, until it is ready to spin itself a hard case, called a pupa. **4** Gradually, it starts to change and soon becomes an adult butterfly.

▽ The death's head hawk moth of Africa gets its name from the skull-shaped pattern on its back.

◁ See for yourself how caterpillars turn into butterflies. Collect some caterpillars and put them in a large jar, along with the branches you found them on. Fasten some net across the top with an elastic band. Add fresh leaves every day and watch the changes as they happen. Make sure you let the butterflies go as soon as they can fly.

Find out more
Bee and Wasp
Cricket and Grasshopper
Insect
Reproduction

Beetle

There are over a quarter of a million species of beetle in the world. They come in many shapes and sizes, but all have one thing in common – a pair of delicate, folded wings protected by a hard outer casing or shell.

△ Some species of water beetle hunt tadpoles and baby fish. Before diving, the beetles come to the surface to collect air under their wing casings.

◁ Fireflies are not flies, but flying beetles that glow in the dark. They give off light from their abdomen (rear body part) to attract mates. They let out short, regular flashes – each species has its own typical flash pattern. In some of the 1,900 species the female does not fly. She is called a glow-worm.

△ Dung beetles collect a ball of dung and lay an egg in it. When the egg hatches, the new beetle larva eats the dung.

▽ Stag beetles are huge, measuring up to 7.5 centimetres long. The males often fight each other with their large jaws.

Find out more
Ant and Termite
Communication
Defence
Fly
Insect

Cricket and Grasshopper

Crickets and grasshoppers are insects that prefer to hop on their long back legs rather than fly. Males 'sing' to attract mates – grasshoppers do this by rubbing their back legs together, while crickets use their wings.

△ Many grasshoppers are brightly coloured. This warns predators that the grasshopper can spit a nasty-tasting protective foam.

△ Locusts are a kind of grasshopper found in Africa. Every now and then they form huge swarms, which destroy crops.

◁ Grasshoppers have very strong muscles in their long back legs and a remarkable spring in their knees. The grasshopper can jump 12 times its own length – this would be like a child jumping over a house!

▽ Bush crickets, like this great green bush cricket, are known as katydids because the male's song sounds like someone saying, 'Katy did'. Females have slit-like ears in their front legs, which they use to listen to the singing males.

Fact box

• Crickets and grasshoppers eat leaves and grasses. Some eat other insects too.
• Each species has its own special song.
• People used to keep crickets in cages to hear them sing.

Find out more
Beetle
Communication
Defence
Insect

Glossary

A **glossary** is a list of useful words. Some of the words used in this book may be new to you. You can find out more about them here.

abdomen the rear part of an insect's body.

ambush to lie in hiding, waiting to attack.

antennae a pair of thin, movable feelers on the heads of insects.

carnivore an animal that eats the meat of other animals.

carrion the rotting remains of a dead animal, often left over after a predator has finished with its kill.

cell the basic unit of life. All living things are made up of cells.

colony a group of animals of the same species that live together closely.

domestic animal an animal that is tame and is used to living near people.

endangered if a species is at risk of dying out it is described as being endangered.

environment the surroundings or the place where an animal lives.

extinct an animal species that has died out is extinct.

herbivore an animal that eats only plants.

invertebrate an animal without a backbone.

kill a dead animal that has been killed by another.

mate a male and female animal mate, or pair up, to reproduce.

nocturnal a nocturnal animal sleeps or rests during the day and comes out at night.

omnivore an animal that eats both plants and meat.

plankton tiny plants and animals that float in seas, rivers and lakes.

predator an animal that kills and eats other animals for food.

prey an animal that is hunted or killed by another animal for food.

rodent a group of small mammals, including rats, with big, sharp front teeth for gnawing.

savanna warm, dry grassland with just a few small trees.

scavenge animals that scavenge do not hunt and kill their own meat, but feed on carrion left behind by predators.

species a particular kind of animal. The animals in a species all look alike and behave in a similar way. Animals can only breed with members of their own species. There are about a million animal species on the Earth.

tropical found in the tropics, which are the warm areas that lie either side of the Earth's equator. Tropical forests are hot and wet.

tundra the flat, treeless land in the Arctic. The ground is so cold here that only a few small plants can grow.

vertebrate an animal with a backbone.

young the offspring, or babies, of adult animals.

Index

This index helps you find subjects in the book. It is in alphabetical order. Main entries are in dark, or **bold**, type

The publisher would like to thank the following for contributing to this book:

Photographs
Page 3, 4 Lyndon Parker; 6–7 Getty Imagebank; 11 Lyndon Parker; 12 Lyndon Parker *t, mr*, Oxford Scientific Films *ml*; 13 Lyndon Parker *t*, Oxford Scientific Films *m*; 14, 16, 17 Lyndon Parker; 18–19 Oxford Scientific Films/Photolibrary.com; 20 Lyndon Parker; 24, 27, 30, 31, 32 Oxford Scientific Films; 33 Andy Teare Photography *t*, Lyndon Parker *b*; 36 Oxford Scientific Films; 38 Lyndon Parker; 41, 43, 46 Oxford Scientific Films; 47, 48 Andy Teare Photography; 50 Oxford Scientific Films; 51 Planet Earth Pictures; 53 Andy Teare Photography; 54, 55 Oxford Scientific Films; 56 Planet Earth Pictures; 57 Oxford Scientific Films; 58 Andy Teare Photography *t*, Oxford Scientific Films *m*; 60 David Aubrey/Science Photo Library; 61 Lyndon Parker *tr*, Andy Teare Photography *tl*; 62, 63 Oxford Scientific Films; 64, 65 Lyndon Parker; 66 Oxford Scientific Films; 67 Andy Teare Photography *t*, Oxford Scientific Films *br*; 68, 72 Oxford Scientific Films; 73 Andy Teare Photography; 74, 75, 76, 77, 78, 79 Lyndon Parker; 80 Oxford Scientific Films; 81 Lyndon Parker; 82–83 Oxford Scientific Films/Photolibrary.com/Mike Powles; 84 Andy Teare Photography; 85 Oxford Scientific Films; 86 Planet Earth Pictures; 87 Andy Teare Photography; 88 Lyndon Parker; 89 Planet Earth Pictures; 90 Planet Earth Pictures *t*, Oxford Scientific Films *m*; 91, 93 Oxford Scientific Films; 94 Lyndon Parker *t*, Oxford Scientific Films *b*; 95, 96 Andy Teare Photography; 98 Planet Earth Pictures; 99 Tony Stone Images *ml*, Oxford Scientific Films *b*; 101 Andy Teare Photography; 102 Oxford Scientific Films; 104–105 Oxford Scientific Films/Photolibrary.com/Creatas; 106 Lyndon Parker; 109 Andy Teare Photography; 110 Oxford Scientific Films; 111 Lyndon Parker; 112 Tony Stone Images; 113 Andy Teare Photography; 116–117 Getty Imagebank; 118, 119 Lyndon Parker; 120, 121, 122 Oxford Scientific Films; 124–125 Oxford Scientific Films/Photolibrary.com/Stefan Mokrzecki; 126 Lyndon Parker; 130, 131 Lyndon Parker; 132, 133, 138 Oxford Scientific Films; 139 Andy Teare Photography; 140 Planet Earth Pictures

Artists
Graham Allen, Norman Arlott, Mike Atkinson, Craig Austin, Peter Barrett, Caroline Bernard, Robin Bouttell (Wildlife Art Agency), Peter Bull, John Butler, Robin Carter (Wildlife Art Agency), Jim Channel, Dan Cole (Wildlife Art Agency), David Cook, Richard Draper, Brin Edwards, Cecelia Fitzsimons (Wildlife Art Agency), Wayne Ford (Wildlife Art Agency), Chris Forsey, Ray Greenway, Nick Hall, Darren Harvey (Wildlife Art Agency), David Holmes, Steve Howes, Mark Iley (Wildlife Art Agency), Ian Jackson (Wildlife Art Agency), Martin Knowelden, Terence Lambert, Mick Loates, Bernard Long, Andrew Macdonald, Alan Male (Linden Artists Ltd), David Marshall, Doreen McGuinness, Brian Mcintyre, G. Melhuish, William Oliver, R.W. Orr, Nicki Palin, Bruce Pearson, Andie Peck (Wildlife Art Agency), Bryan Poole, Clive Pritchard (Wildlife Art Agency), John Rignall (Linden Artists Ltd), Steve Roberts (Wildlife Art Agency), Bernard Robinsons, Eric Robson (Garden Studio Illustrators' Agents), G. Robson, Mike L. Rowe (Wildlife Art Agency), Peter David Scott (Wildlife Art Agency), Guy Smith (Mainline Design), M. Stewart (Wildlife Art Agency), Mike Taylor (Garden Studio Illustrators' Agents), Joan Thompson, Treve Tamblin, Guy Troughton, Wendy Webb, Lynne Wells (Wildlife Art Agency), David Whatmore, Ann Winterbottom, David Wood (Wildlife Art Agency), David Wright, T. K. Wayte (David Lewis Management)

Models
Zak Broscombe Walker, Kechet Buckle Zetty, Martha Button, Jennifer Ching, Yazmina Faiz, Ellie French, Jonathan Hodgson, Christopher Jones, Ellie Kemp, Peter Kemp, Daniel MacArthur Seal, Jack Nazareth, Jamie Nazareth, Julia Nazareth, Iynn-ade Odedina, Okikade Odedina, Michael Rego, Rudi Russell, Leila Sowahan